Winds of C

Alcalá de los Gazules
in the 20th Century

… (the levante) is a strange uncomfortable wind for those who don't know it. But living here, you have to learn to live with it, to love it even. If you hate it, you are lost; it will drive you to despair and drive you mad when it blows day after day without stopping.

(Miguel de Donlebún Quijado)

The levante isn't only in our head, it's an essential part of our language – depending on its strength we call it levante, levantera or levantazo … hot and dry, the wind of fires. Then comes the poniente, cool, clear and refreshing, the countryside breathes again…

(José Luengo)

"El levante las mueve y el poniente las llueve"

(local saying)

Contents

For Inma

Introduction

Alcalá de los Gazules looks from a distance like someone has emptied a box of sparkling white sugar cubes into a wilderness of green forests, golden meadows and silver peaks. It sits in the middle of the Province of Cádiz, in the south-west corner of Spain. As well as an urban nucleus of around two thousand tightly-packed dwellings clinging to the hillside, the municipality includes over 480 km^2 of undulating farmland to the west and tree-covered uplands to the east (most of which now lie within the Alcornocales Natural Park).

Alcalá has been settled for at least two thousand years – the Romans, the Visigoths, the Moors and the French all came and went, leaving their mark on the landscape. Its name comes from the Arabic Al Qalat (the castle); "Gazules" is a little more controversial but probably relates to a Berber tribe called Gazies. The most recent invaders, though few in number, started arriving from northern Europe at the start of the 21st century in search of a quality of life increasingly difficult to attain in the modern world. I am one of them.

For a town of its size (5,500) Alcalá attracts a fierce loyalty among its natives, especially those who left long ago to look for work. They come home for every fair and festival, trundling their suitcases over the cobbles; they write eulogies and verses in the town's annual magazine or on its Facebook pages; there is even a street corner named for them (Plazuela de los Emigrantes). Alcalá has a strong sense of civic pride, tradition, solidarity and community that is soon evident to the incomer, but regarded as perfectly normal by those who grew up here.

The 20th century saw massive social change in Alcalá. It began with the almost feudal system of land ownership and peasant labour, followed in the early 1930s by short-lived hopes of social justice during the Second Republic. Then came the brutality of the Nationalist coup d'état in 1936, forty years of fascist dictatorship, and depopulation resulting from economic changes in the 1960s. The transition to democracy in the late 1970s culminated in a new Constitution guaranteeing universal rights, and a centre-left government during the 1980s which invested heavily in health and education. In the 1990s Spain's membership of the European Union and the designation of the Alcornocales Natural Park led to further changes in the local economy.

The book is chronological and is divided into five chapters. Each one begins with some brief background information on the political and economic situation of the country as a whole during the period covered in the chapter, before looking at specific aspects of Alcalá daily life such as employment, social movements, urban development, fairs and festivals, education and health. Sources referred to in the text are listed at the end of the book.

Alcalá in the late 1960s

Acknowledgements

Although many people have written about Alcalá over the years there is virtually nothing in English, so I have translated material from a range of sources to try and produce a coherent history of the town during the 20th century. In particular I have been inspired and informed by the writings of Carlos Perales Pizarro, Agustín Coca Pérez, Ismael Almagro Montes de Oca, Jerome Mintz, Jaime Guerra, Guillermo García Jiménez, Paco Pizarro, Juan Leiva, Francisco Teodoro Sánchez Vera and most recently, Juan Pedro Romero Benítez, saviour of Alcalá's priceless municipal archive.

The blog *Historia de Alcalá de los Gazules* was an invaluable source, as were the annual publications produced by the Ayuntamiento, *Apuntes Históricos y de Nuestro Patrimonio*.

I must also thank numerous friends and neighbours who, if they were puzzled by my insistence on knowing what they did when they were teenagers or what their mothers had in their kitchens, were far too polite to say so.

Thanks also to Bob Lloyd for moral support beyond the call of duty, John Cantelo for a first-rate copy-editing service, Tony Pearce for pointing out certain deficiencies, and Helen Rigby for a Whatsapp out of the blue telling me I ought to write a book.

Terminology

There are some words that don't translate well into English, or have more than one meaning, so I have kept them in their original form:

- *Alcalaíno/a:* a native of Alcalá de los Gazules.
- *Ayuntamiento:* the municipal council (elected representatives and employees) and the town hall building.
- *Campo:* field or countryside - a place of work, a source of food, and more recently a location for leisure activities.
- *Campesino/a:* a peasant or farmer - someone who lives and works in the campo.
- *Carbonero:* a maker of *carbón vegetal* (charcoal), the primary fuel for cooking and heating until the 1960s.
- *Corchero*: a worker involved in harvesting the bark of the cork-oak, which is sold on for commercial cork production.
- *Finca*: a country house, estate or farm, or a large urban property.
- *Ganadero:* someone who looks after livestock, either his own or, more usually, on behalf of landowners.
- *Jornalero:* a worker hired at a daily rate to do seasonal jobs such as ploughing or harvesting crops.
- *Latifundismo:* a system of land ownership involving large estates whose owners usually live elsewhere.
- *Montes:* hilly or mountainous terrain covered in trees or scrub, usually uncultivated but used for grazing, foraging or hunting.
- *Pueblo:* literally "town" or "people" - Alcalá has the status of *ciudad* (city) for historical reasons, but the locals refer to it as the pueblo and that includes the inhabitants as well as the buildings.
- *Ranchero:* a small landowner or tenant farmer, living on and farming his own land.

Acronyms used in this book

Political parties

CEDA: Confederación Española de Derechas Autónomas (right-wing coalition formed during the Second Republic)

FE-JONS: Falange Española de las Juntas de Ofensiva Nacional Sindicalista (fascist organisation founded in 1934, the only party permitted during Franco's dictatorship)

PCE: Partido Comunista de España (Spanish Communist Party)

UCD: Unión de Centro Democrático (centre-right party that governed from 1977 to 1981)

PSOE: Partido Socialista Obrero Español (Spanish Socialist Workers' Party)

PP: Partido Popular (People's Party, eventual successor to UCD)

Workers' movements and trades unions

CNT: Confederacíon Nacional de Trabajo (confederation of anarchosyndicalist unions)

FAI: Federación Anarquista Ibérica (radical sub-section of CNT)

CC-OO: Comisiones Obreras (Workers' Commissions, originally affiliated to the PCE)

UGT: Unión General de Trabajadores (General Workers' Union, affiliated to the PSOE)

CNS: Central Obrera Nacional-Sindicalista (the only union permitted during the Franco regime)

Government programmes and agencies

EC: Empleo Comunitario (community employment programme)

ICONA: Instituto para la Conservación de la Naturaleza (Nature Conservation Institute)

PER: Plan de Empleo Rural (successor to EC)

VPO: Vivienda de Protección Oficial (subsidised housing)

Miscellaneous

PNA: Parque Natural de los Alcornocales

Pts: pesetas

SAFA: Fundación Escuelas Profesionales de la Sagrada Familia

SEAT: Sociedad Española de Automóviles de Turismo

CHAPTER 1 – 1900-1930

"Hygiene in this town is not as good as it should be, with a growing population, still lacking sewers in most streets; these are narrow and winding, the squares are few and small, the houses are low, small and most with no back yard, with many rooms below ground and shared with neighbours and animals ..." (Official medical report on Alcalá de los Gazules in 1901)

Background

The period covered in this chapter began with a false democracy and ended with a flaky dictatorship. Neither regime did much to improve the lot of the working-class in Andalucía.

After the restoration of the Bourbon monarchy in 1874 Spain was governed by a deliberate rotation of Liberals and Conservatives known as the *Turno Pacífico*, based on the English bipartisan model, in an attempt to ensure stability in the country. Both parties supported the monarchy and the interests of the middle and upper classes. Other parties were excluded from the rotation. The system depended on a chain of command from central government via the provincial governors to a network of local bosses called *caciques*, who would instruct the electorate (sometimes by violent means) which party they were to vote for. This applied to local as well as national elections.

This system was brought to an end in 1923 by a military coup led by General Miguel Primo de Rivera, an aristocrat born in Jerez de la Frontera. He grew up as part of what British historian Gerald Brenan called "a hard-drinking, whoring, horse-loving aristocracy" that ruled "over the most starved and down-trodden race of agricultural labourers in Europe." A self-proclaimed patriot, he believed that politicians were the ruin of Spain and he could do a better job on his own, modernising the economy and investing in infrastructure. After the coup he made himself president, declared martial law and replaced provincial politicians with military officers. He raised taxes and borrowed money to pay for public works, but ended up losing the support of the army and the king. Having done nothing to cultivate a base of popular support in the country, he was obliged to resign in January 1930 and died a few weeks later.

During most of this period Spain was fighting a succession of wars in North Africa, where it was keen to expand its influence following the loss of its last remaining colonies to the USA. In 1908 it signed a deal with a tribal leader to exploit mines around the coastal enclave of Melilla, but these were attacked by fighters from other tribes. This led to years of conflict. Spain had no professional army and relied on poorly trained conscripts who stood little chance against the guerrilla tactics of the Africans, resulting in much loss of life. The wars finally ended in 1927, with the assistance of the French.

Alcalá de los Gazules, early 20th century

Municipal byelaws of 1900

In 1900 the Ayuntamiento of Alcalá de los Gazules produced a set of byelaws[1] covering over two hundred topics, ranging from fairs and festivals to street-cleaning and fire-fighting. They offer a vivid picture of daily life in the pueblo at the turn of the century:

Public entertainment
For the three days of Carnival, fancy dress may be worn in the streets until 10 p.m. provided it does not imitate the uniforms or robes worn by state officials or priests. No weapons or any kind of dangerous object must be carried while wearing fancy dress, even if they are part of the costume. Fireworks are banned, as are

molesting the ladies and throwing dirty water on people in a way which might damage or stain their clothes.

Good management of festivals and religious solemnities

From Holy Thursday until the following Saturday, out of respect for the religious beliefs of the Spanish people, the owners of establishments selling alcohol who leave their doors open must not allow any kind of noise to be heard on the street. Street-vendors must not announce their wares, and people must not assemble in church doorways in a way which could hamper the entry and exit of the faithful.

Meeting places

Cafes, bars and billiard halls may stay open until midnight, provided that noise doesn't disturb the neighbours. Once closed, the owners must not sell drinks through windows or shutters except in cases of recognised emergency. Games of chance are strictly prohibited.

Bull-runs

No bullocks may be run in the streets without the permission of the authorities. Organisers must prepare the site at their own expense under the direction of the Ayuntamiento, and close off all side-streets to avoid any risk to persons or property. Animals must be kept in a safe place before and after the event, and must not be ill-treated. The local authority will co-operate as far as possible with the organisers, bearing in mind that these events should not be held to make a profit, but to provide entertainment for the people.

Theatres

All shows must take place at the time advertised on the posters, at the advertised prices. There must be no distinction of class or other category. Smoking may only take place in the corridors outside the theatre. From the moment the curtain is raised, the audience must remain seated so others can see the show without obstruction. Groups of people should avoid blocking stairways and exits at the end of the event.

Pot-banging and noise

It is prohibited to make a noise in the streets during the night in a way that might disturb the rest of the neighbours. This includes gathering in gangs, musical serenades, and the banging of pots and pans.

Begging

In order to ask for alms or appeal to public charity, a licence must be obtained from the mayor. Licences will only be valid for the period judged necessary, and will not be granted to people from outside the town. Anyone finding a lost or abandoned child must take him to the town hall where he will be given a meal. The authorities will make all efforts to locate the parents or guardians.

Road safety and carriages

All carriages, carts and wagons entering or leaving the town must be preceded by someone on foot, who will be obliged to carry a lantern during the hours of darkness. Vehicles transporting goods must not block the way of pedestrians and should load or unload their goods as quickly as possible. When two vehicles meet in a narrow street, a loaded cart will take priority over an empty one. If they are both in the same condition, the one nearest a corner or coming uphill will back up.

Beasts of burden

Horse-racing in the streets or public open spaces is expressly prohibited. It is forbidden to tether animals in the streets in a way that might frighten or inconvenience the public, or to hurt or ill-treat them in any way, including overloading them. Blacksmiths and vets must only exercise their profession in designated places, so as not to inconvenience the public. Deliverers of water, firewood, straw or charcoal must use only the wider streets and not block the passage of passers-by by mounting the pavements. Drivers must refrain from using bad language that might offend public decency.

Dogs

Mastiffs and hunting dogs must not be kept in the town, and if passing through, must be kept on a lead or chain and wear a muzzle. Other kinds of dog must wear a collar with the name and address of the owner. Any dog found on the street not wearing a collar will be taken to a pound. The owner may reclaim it within 24 hours on payment of a fine. Those not reclaimed will be put down. Anyone finding a dog suffering from rabies is permitted to kill it.

Behaviour of youngsters

Within the town, youths are prohibited from fighting, playing ballgames and letting off bangers, throwing rockets and dead animals, or anything else that could offend passers-by or damage their clothes. Anyone found breaking these rules may be detained for two days or their parents fined 5 pesetas.

Fire precautions

Domestic fireplaces must be set in the main walls of the dwelling and chimneys must open at a higher level than neighbouring roofs. They must not be placed in walls adjoining other properties without the consent of the neighbour. Fires must not be lit in court-yards. Braziers must not be lit on balconies and ashes must not be thrown onto the street.

Dangerous establishments

The establishment within the town of factories producing fire-works, gunpowder or matches is prohibited. Tar, dried fish, resin, matches and other flammable materials must only be sold by authorised persons, who must exercise vigilance to prevent fires. The wholesale storage of said materials, as well as coal, firewood, straw and other fuels, should if possible be located in isolated places on the outskirts of the town. These places must not be entered at night, even with a lamp, and smoking is prohibited there at all times.

Fire prevention measures

The mayor is responsible for ensuring that all fires are put out, giving orders to municipal employees and members of the public if necessary. Anyone noticing a fire must alert the authorities imme-diately, and a bell will ring until the danger is over. If a fire occurs at night, the municipal guards will announce in a loud voice the place of the occurrence. All residents are required to make water from their wells available to help extinguish fires. Water-bearers must provide the services of themselves and their animals when required to do so.

Street-lighting

All streets and squares will be illuminated at the Ayuntamiento's expense until midnight on the twenty-two days each month when there is no moonlight. The lights will remain on until dawn at the entrances to the churches, the prison and the HQ of the Guardia Civil, and during public festivals.

Water-bearers and public wells

The office of water-bearer is open to anyone, provided they obtain a licence from the mayor. The Ayuntamiento will nominate a guard for each of the public wells, someone honest and of good conduct. The guards will ensure that the wells are kept clean and in good order, preventing people from throwing in sticks, stones, dead animals or other contaminants. People who go to the wells to collect water, either for themselves or for distribution to others, must fill their respective vessels in the order of arrival. The guards will make sure everyone keeps to their turn and resolve any disputes.

Bread

The manufacture and sale of bread in this town is open to anyone, provided they advise the authorities. Bread for public sale must be made with good quality wheat flour not mixed with any other substance, well kneaded and properly baked. Loaves will be sold in standard sizes ranging from 460g to 1380g, and anyone who feels they have been swindled should report the baker to the authorities who will take steps to rectify the matter. The mayor will arrange for regular inspections of baking premises to ensure good standards of cleanliness and quality.

Meat

All animals whose meat is to be sold for public consumption must be taken to the abattoir for slaughter, where they will be inspected and their condition and brands noted. No animal destined for slaughter will be run, beaten or mishandled, but must be sacrificed peacefully, not via blows with sticks or rocks, or killed by dogs, but with instruments designed for the purpose. The slaughter must take place on the same day they arrive. Animals taken to the abattoir must be alive and healthy, with no recent injuries caused by dogs, wolves or other carnivores. Dead, injured or sick beasts must be disposed of by burning. No animal shall be killed clandestinely; only the public slaughterer may do this job. Nonetheless, individuals may kill their own pigs at home for their own consumption.

Meat on sale to the public must be clearly labelled and priced, with different kinds separated by a board. The sale of rotten meat or meat from infected animals is strictly forbidden.

Public slaughterhouse on Calle Nuestra Señora de los Santos

A divided society

Alcalá began the century with a population of 8,877, rising to 9,508 by 1930. It prospered under the economic stability resulting from the *Turno Pacífico*, and was the envy of other towns in the district because of the wide range of cultural opportunities available; there were social clubs for craftsmen, conservatives, liberals, labourers, teachers, olive-growers, merchants, businessmen and wine-producers (sadly, Alcalá's vineyards were wiped out by phylloxera aphids at the beginning of the 20th century). Residents could get whatever they needed without leaving the pueblo. It had three pharmacies and six doctors, four olive-oil merchants, six shoe-makers, six millers, four schoolteachers, nine haberdasheries, two fabric shops, two hat-makers, several barbers, countless bars selling wine and brandy, various bakers, greengrocers and butchers, and numerous *tiendas de ultramarinos*, so-called because they sold goods imported from overseas.[2]

But society was deeply divided. The majority of the wealthy inhabitants lived in the Calle Real in large houses, some with their own patio and well. The middle-classes were more scattered, but in acceptable houses. The poor lived mainly in the higher part of the town, in large crumbling fincas around the Plaza Alta. Within these buildings entire families often lived in one room divided by a curtain, on one side of which was the bedroom and on the other the living area; cooking was done in a pot over a charcoal fire (*fogón*) in a communal patio, there was no running water or electricity, and sanitary conditions were rudimentary.[3]

Outside the urban area, where half the population lived at that time, the rancheros and tenant farmers lived in fincas or *cortijos* on their land. For the campesinos who owned no land the most typical dwelling was a *choza*, a one-roomed shack made from earth and reeds built alongside cattle-trails or on the edge of the estates where they worked. The landowner usually allowed them to have a small vegetable garden and maybe a pig and some chickens. They burned charcoal for cooking and heating, and given the nature of the dwellings, fires were not infrequent, often leading to fatalities.[4]

Alcalá ladies, 1909

Working-class dwellings near the Plaza Alta

Chozas on the outskirts of Alcalá, c.1930

Land ownership[5]

For the majority of alcalaínos, employment opportunities were seasonal, scarce and poorly paid. The system of land ownership played a major part in the perpetuation of rural poverty.

The privately-owned land around Alcalá consisted mainly of large estates owned by the nobility and handed down over the centuries, in a system known as latifundismo. None of the landowners lived in the pueblo and very few lived on their estates, only visiting them for the occasional hunting party.

Some of these latifundistas leased parts of their estates to tenant farmers who would plant crops, graze cattle or divide the land into smaller units to rent out for a profit. There was also a class of small-scale farmers who owned and lived on their land, known as rancheros. It was in the interests of both leaseholders and rancheros to cultivate the land intensively rather than leaving it idle for hunting. They would employ workers on a daily or seasonal basis for specific tasks, working alongside them in the fields and generally treating them better than the absentee land-lords did.

Publicly-owned land around towns like Alcalá, known as *montes propios,* had for centuries been used by residents for grow-ing fruit and vegetables, grazing livestock, foraging, collecting wood, hunting birds and animals for food, and making charcoal. In return they had certain responsibilities, such as constructing firebreaks and keeping water sources clean. In addition to the *montes propios,* land owned by the Church and the nobility was traditionally leased at low rents to tenant farmers for grazing or cultivation. But much of this municipal and Church-owned land was sold off to private buyers during the 19th and early 20th centuries in a process known as *desamortización,* an attempt by the national government to democratise land-ownership and build a prosperous middle-class, while at the same time using the revenues to pay off the national debt and finance public works.

Alcalá lost more than two-thirds of its public land this way, depriving many people of their livelihood. Instead of democrat-ising the ownership of land, one particular individual who had connections with the Ayuntamiento ended up with the lion's share.[6] He needed to recoup the cost as quickly as possible. Grazing rights, once free, were auctioned to the highest bidder. The campesinos had to pay rent for land that had previously been public, and pay for the right to collect firewood and make charcoal.

Trades and crafts

The same trades and jobs existed in Alcalá as in any other pueblo – shopkeepers, waiters, public officials, tailors, shoe-makers, security forces, domestic servants and so on - but Alcalá, due to its location on the edge of an extensive forest, had its own specialised trades as well.

Corcheros

During the summer months many men worked on the cork harvest. The cork-oak forest in the Alcornocales Natural Park is one of the largest in Europe (*alcornoque* is the Spanish word for this tree, but the locals call them *chaparros*). The industry took off at the end of the 17th century when the wine producers around Jerez de la Frontera started to use corks in their bottles.

The corcheros worked in teams known as *cuadrillas*, each with a foreman and their own cook. They worked, ate and slept out in the cork groves, only returning to the pueblo every two weeks to see their families and change their clothes. Corcheros then, as now, took great care of their axes and other tools. Removing the bark to obtain the cork is highly skilled work, as it can only be harvested from a tree every nine years or so, and great care must be taken not to damage the "mother layer" beneath the bark from which the next crop will grow.

The process has not changed much over the years. Once removed from the tree the slabs of bark are loaded onto the backs of mules and taken to open-air *patios* where they are weighed, stacked up and stored for several weeks. The slabs are then boiled in tanks to remove impurities and improve their elasticity. The next stage is careful scraping and trimming, after which the cork is graded for quality, and finally the boards are pressed and baled before being transported to the town.

Although no commercial manufacture of cork products took place in Alcalá, people made use of it in their daily lives:

> *... baskets for keeping bread; washboards - large, curved pieces of cork to scrub clothes on; cork boards put in front of the table or the bed to keep in the heat, or in front of the fire to catch the sparks; lids for jars, bottles and jugs; thin layers of cork for packaging; toys and balls for children to play with; cork wall-linings to soundproof rooms; pistol shot for children's toy guns; lifebelts for learning to swim; all kinds of floats to hold up the fishing nets used by the tuna fleets, and a thousand other uses.* [7]

Carboneros

Charcoal (*carbón vegetal*) was a major source of income from October to May each year, when the cork season was over and fewer hands were needed for agricultural tasks. Before the arrival of gas and electricity charcoal was used extensively for cooking and heating, and even sent to the ports of Cádiz and Algeciras for use on steamships.

The carboneros first cleared the forests and grazing areas of low-lying shrubs, brushwood, roots and fallen branches.

> *Then the oven would be constructed on a piece of clean, flat ground, where a curved base was set up. The armaero arranged the oven, starting with two parallel trunks on which the wood was criss-crossed; the smallest bits were placed nearest the entrance to start the fire going. Then they built the sides and 'shoulders', then the back part, and finally the crown or top part. Next they prepared the kindling, using twigs of* lentisco *laid out in a fan-shape and covered with firewood. Then they would cover it all with earth, using panniers to raise it off the kindling, and leaving an opening at the front part with two tubes to permit the passage of air. They then lit the fire in the opening, where the smallest twigs were. The fire would go right up into the crown of the oven. The front part of the oven would cave in, and they would cover the holes with more earth. Eventually the fire would die down and they would use thin poles to make air-holes. The fire would be drawn to the rear of the oven and the cooking process would be finalised. It only remained to take off the baked earth, remove the charcoal and pile it up. Finally the muleteers would load it into their panniers or wrap it up in sacks ready to sell.[7]*

The carboneros were either self-employed (often working in family groups) or worked in teams hired on a daily rate. The former had to pay the landowners for the privilege of clearing their land, but kept the profits; they usually worked in shifts day and night without a break. The latter worked from sunrise to sunset and were paid at the end of their shift every two weeks, when they would return to the pueblo.

The charcoal was transported into town on the backs of mules to a loading dock behind the Peña de Carbón, the large slab of volcanic rock to the west of the town centre. It was weighed and purchased by trusted intermediaries, then sold on to buyers. By 1930 lorries were used for the onward journey, but mules were still used to bring the fuel into Alcalá.

Arrieros

Caring for the mules that played such a vital part in the local economy was a year-round job for both the muleteers (*arrieros*) and their wives and children.

The dialogue with the animal starts from childhood and never ends. The job involves pampering and caring for the animal. It eats before you do, you love it as if it were part of the family, you must care for it whether it is working or not, and be as attentive to it as if it were a child ... Inside every arriero *is a surgeon, a vet, a healer who knows about remedies, herbs and potions. He is also a blacksmith and a saddler, always ready to do a repair job out in the forest. He is an expert at finding his way around the densest woodland by day or night, with or without moonlight. He knows about knots and packing, and a thousand ways to load up the cargo ... He knows about contracts and business deals, reaching agreements in good times and bad, and has a family which extends beyond the home, forming a network of solidarity and mutual help among comrades ...*[8]

Other specialist trades included making the wicker baskets used for transporting goods, numerous wooden items from cartwheels to axe handles and *dornillos* (large wooden bowls used for making gazpacho, the staple food of campo workers). The *latero* made and repaired tin pots and pans; the *calero* quarried and refined lime to whitewash the buildings; the *afilador* announced his arrival by playing a flute, upon which people would bring out their knives and tools for him to sharpen. Then there were shearers, blacksmiths, well-diggers (some of whom apparently had the gift of water-divining), drovers, chair-makers, soap-makers...[7]

Agriculture

While the wooded uplands to the east of the town provided cork, charcoal and firewood, much of the flatter land within the Alcalá municipality was used for arable farming, based on the three-field/three-year rotation system. One-third of the land was left for pasture, fertilised with manure from grazing animals. The second year it was tilled and planted with nitrate-producing legumes, usually chickpeas, lentils or beans, and in the final year it was planted with wheat or other cereals. The whole cycle would begin again after the harvest. Oxen, mules and cows were used for ploughing and sowing.[5]

Ganaderos

Livestock breeders played an essential role in the agricultural cycle and were employed on an annual basis by landowners. On 29th September, the day of San Miguel (Michaelmas), they were paid for the year's work and hired for a further year. If there was any dispute the contract might not be renewed and they and their families would be homeless, forced to pack their belongings onto the backs of their animals and head off in search of a post elsewhere.[6]

Agricultural workers

There were various classes of agricultural worker. *Rancheros* were at the top of the hierarchy, as they owned the land they worked. They built solid two-storey houses, living on the ground floor and storing grain upstairs. *Colonos* rented land and had contracts of between two and ten years, renewable at Michaelmas. *Aparceros* worked the land and shared the harvest equally with the owners. *Pelaos* lived on small farmsteads whose leases passed from father to son, and the whole family would assist with growing crops and raising animals. *Yunteros* owned a pair or two of oxen and would hire themselves out to the landowners. They usually lived in *chozas* (reed huts) by the side of the *cañadas* (cattle trails) where their children might raise turkeys or other animals that grazed alongside the oxen. *Pegujaleros* rented the less fertile rocky lands and paid their rent in wheat.

Near the bottom of the hierarchy was the *jornalero*, who was hired for short-term contracts as required and paid a daily rate. Those employed near the town walked to and from work, but for lands further away they slept in *gañanias*, rough bunkhouses sleeping up to thirty men. They returned home every ten days or so for a change of clothing. If they worked for twenty consecutive days they were entitled to a day off (without pay).

> *During the winter ploughing the men in the* gañanias *rose well before dawn, prepared coffee, then went to harness the animals for the day's work. There was a break for a cigarette at 8.00 a.m., a gazpacho at 9.00, another meal at 1.00 p.m., two more short rest periods in the afternoon,*

and at 6 p.m. the men returned to the gañania *or to their homes. In the* gañanias *the workers continued their tasks after dusk by the light of an oil lamp, weaving baskets from palm leaves to hold the threshed grain.*[9]

In the summer months during the harvest they slept outside. The reapers (*segadores*) generally worked a season of forty days, sunrise to sunset. Each contract might take three days. It was tortuous work, especially when the notorious Levante was blowing from the east. Each team of ten men received a ration of 10kg of bread and one litre of oil a day, with 2.5kg of chickpeas every ten days, along with some vinegar and salt. Alcalá's famous *gazpacho caliente* started off as campo breakfast; stale bread soaked in hot water then mixed to a paste with olive oil, vinegar and salt in the *dornillo*. The workers would all eat from the *dornillo* using their own spoons. Midday gazpacho might include tomatoes, onions and cucumbers.

At the bottom of the economic scale with virtually no secure employment were the *eventuales*, hired on a daily basis for unskilled jobs such as sowing, weeding and helping with the harvest. They would go to the Alameda early in the morning and see if there was work available. When the weather was bad they did not work and they did not get paid. On average they worked about six months of the year. Even when working, the wages did not feed a family. A loaf of bread cost the equivalent of half a day's pay.

When there was no work they relied on relatives or obtained credit at the local store. They would forage in the countryside for whatever was in season; prickly pears, snails, wild asparagus, edible thistles and the occasional rabbit, either for their own consumption or to sell. Songbirds were trapped using sticky lime on the branches where they perched. If a poacher was caught he would lose his catch and his traps and face a stiff fine.

Women did not work in the fields during this period. Some worked as seamstresses, or raised hens and sold the eggs. Many families kept pigs, which were slaughtered in November and gave them protein through the winter months in the form of hams, chorizos or other types of sausage, which were hung from hooks in the ceiling. Children helped to supplement the family income, guarding livestock, weeding the crops and picking up stones, or sent into domestic service. Few had the opportunity to attend school and most were illiterate.[6]

Social reform

In 1903 the Institute of Social Reform was created with the objective of improving labour relations and acting as mediator in case of conflict between employers and workers. In Alcalá the activities of the local board were mainly restricted to appointing its own members, with one exception: in 1924 the board met with representatives of all the guilds and unions in the town and came up with a set of regulations on opening hours, designed to ensure that workers would not be prevented from attending mass or enjoying free time during festivals. They also established an eight-hour day for workers, unless they came to an agreement with their employers in which case overtime had to be paid.[10]

Public services and utilities

Transport

The first paved road outside the town centre, joining Alcalá and Medina Sidonia, was completed in 1908. From Medina one could access other towns in the province. That same year there was a proposal to build a railway line between Algeciras and San Fernando, passing through Alcalá. This generated great excitement in the town as the only link to the outside world was a horse-drawn coach service to Cádiz, no improvement since Roman times. But in 1913, despite the best efforts of the mayor, the plan was shelved.

In 1927 the bus company Comes began a service from Cádiz to La Linea, passing through Alcalá, and by 1930 there was a daily service to and from Seville known as "la Valenciana", which also brought mail and newspapers.

Water

A few residents had their own water supply, either a well in their patio or water piped in from Las Regajales in the mountains to the north-east of the town, which was expensive. For the rest, women took earthenware jugs to the public fountains and queued to fill them, or if they could afford it purchased water from *agueros* who would deliver it by donkey cart.

There were eight public water sources in the town, several of which were originally built during Moorish times. The Fuente de la Salada, Pozo de Abajo, Pozo de Enmedio and Pozo de Arriba are still in place today; the Fuente de la Alameda, Fuente de las Viñas, Fuente del Rabilero and Pillar del Valle are long gone.

On moonlit nights young men would take their guitars and serenade the girls queuing to fill their containers at the Pozo de Arriba, making a social occasion of the long wait.[6]

Queueing for water at Pozo Arriba

Electricity

The first electricity in the town was the result of a venture in 1906 by the owner of a flour mill, Manuel Nuche Dolarea, using surplus energy from the mill to generate power. The Ayuntamiento provided a site for the facilities needed, to the south of what is now the Paseo de la Playa, and by 1908 the Fábrica Eléctrica Nuestra Señora de los Santos was generating enough electricity to power street-lights from sunset until midnight, as well as illuminations for festivals. This replaced the old carbide lighting which was only available for a few hours on moonless nights.

Gradually individuals and businesses started to subscribe to the service and in 1926 the installations were upgraded. A diesel combustion engine and belt-driven dynamo were installed, extending the number of illuminated streets and enabling the lights to stay on all night.

> ... *From then on, every time the light went out and it was necessary to start the engine again they had to wait for all the town's shoemakers to assemble at the power station, pull on the belt and restart the generator. They had assumed this privilege in exchange for a generous payment in the form of Chiclana wine.*[11]

The electricity factory

Communications

Alcalá had its first post office in 1876, the same year that it was designated a city (*ciudad*) as opposed to a town (*villa*). A telegraph service was available from 1892. There were various public and private telephone networks in Spain at the beginning of the century but the service did not reach Alcalá until 1929. Primo de Rivera nationalised these networks in 1924, forming the Compañía Telefónica Nacional de España (universally known as Telefónica), which incorporated the existing telegraphic infrastructure and extended the telephone service across the country.

Public spaces

José Galán Caballero, mayor in 1901-02, presided over several public investment projects to provide employment and improve the town's physical and social infrastructure: the paving of certain streets; improvements to public fountains; a night school for adults; the creation of a musical band, and the enclosure and refurbishment of a wooded area with a stream running through it at the end of Calle los Pozos, providing benches, potted plants and street-lighting, for use by the public. It was named Parque Galán Caballero when he retired due to ill health in 1902, but subsequently suffered from neglect and vandalism, and the site was used in the 1940s for building a new school.

The open space we now know as the Alameda de la Cruz, then called Plaza de Montes de Oca, was also refurbished at this time. The iron clock in the centre of the Alameda was installed in 1926, when the pace of life was considered to have accelerated to the point where the public needed to know what time it was.

The Gazul Cinema

The first cinema in Alcalá was built in 1928 behind what is now the municipal park. It had wooden benches, cork-lined walls and smelled of bleach. There was only one projector, so the films would be interrupted several times to change the reel.[12]

The street market

The indoor market was not built until the 1930s, but there was a daily market on La Plazuela, at the opposite end of Calle Real from the Alameda. Vendors set up their stalls in the street for the sale of fish and meat, and campesinos sold their produce from baskets. With increased street traffic, as well as the lack of sanitation at a time when typhoid was common, there growing concern about its location. In 1909 an architect was commissioned to design a proper indoor market to be located at the bottom of Calle Rio Verde, but the project was never realised.

Street market in la Plazuela

The nightwatchman

There were few clocks in those days and at 10 p.m. (11 p.m. in summer) a whistle was blown, reminding children playing in the streets and men drinking in the bars that it was time to go home. Then a nightwatchman known as a *sereno* would literally sing the time and the weather conditions, on the hour, until dawn: *"Ave María purísima, las doce y sereno!"* (*sereno* if the weather was calm, *lloviendo* if it was raining, etc.).[6]

Education

At the beginning of the 20th century there were several public schools in Alcalá but they were cramped and unhygienic, catered only for boys, and suffered from shortages of both teachers and materials. Absenteeism was high because children were needed to help their parents on the land. To help alleviate the situation one of the schools began offering an evening class in 1901 and a class for girls was set up in 1907, but they both suffered the same problem: a chronic lack of resources. In 1909 the Ayuntamiento commissioned an architect to draw up plans for a single unified public school for both sexes to be built on Calle Nuestra Señora de los Santos, but due to lack of funds it was never built. Meanwhile the other public schools gradually fell into disrepair and closed.[13]

The Beaterio de Jésus, María y José, located next to the church on the Plaza Alta and run by nuns, was founded by a priest, Diego Angel de Viera, in the 18ᵗʰ century. In 1917, when visited by a reporter from the Diario de Cádiz, it was offering free education to over 120 girls "regardless of social class":

How to describe the unselfish work of this handful of lambs of our Lord? The Beaterio is home to everyone, its doors are open to the fine lady and the humble villager ... Over and over they moulded their souls in the melting-pot of the convent, in which the Sisters were loving mothers to them, and under whose exquisite tender care they emerged winged from the chrysalis, ready to be model mothers and wives.[14]

Diego Valle, socialist and founder of Alcalá's short-lived adult literacy project *Escuela Regeneración* in 1888, took a rather different view:

...Education of women is undertaken by the Holy Mothers of the Sweet Heart of Jesus, whose establishment takes in all the young girls who have no resources to access any other form of education. At barely 15 years old they leave this sanctimonious place impregnated with religious fanaticism, deaf to humanitarian sentiments, and implacable enemies of the world and of the family. The consequence of this appalling moral organisation is the ignorance of the working class of Alcalá who, unaware of the causes of their ills, continue to roll down the fatal slope on which religious sectarians have placed them.[15]

The only other option for education was offered by a handful of teachers giving classes in their own homes. One of them was Manuel Marchante Romero, who taught in Alcalá from 1915 to 1956. In 1930 he wrote to the Cádiz newspaper *El Faro* denouncing the state of education in the town:

> *Many towns in recent years ... have built magnificent schools, modern and hygienic, with advanced teaching methods ... Unfortunately this has not happened in [Alcalá] ... we must recognise as a painful but indisputable reality that we have been guilty of neglect in this respect.*

> *The school I have the honour of running is installed in a place that lacks hygiene and teaching facilities. The children must enter through a narrow corridor stacked with goods, through a slippery communal courtyard where the single classroom door is located. As well as these inconveniences they have to put up with inevitable noise from the neighbours which interrupts their schoolwork and disrupts the order of the classroom.*

> *Due to the small space and shortage of furniture the children have to squeeze onto the ancient benches ... the ceiling is only 2.5 metres high so that when one hundred children are present the air quickly becomes foul, along with the emanations of the toilet located in the premises and the ever-present dust - is there any greater danger to the health of children? ... It is also regrettable that the school lacks any outdoor playground, so there is no opportunity for physical education.*

Marchante proposed constructing a purpose-built school on the site of the Parque Galán Caballero, but this would not come to fruition for another 20 years.[13]

Health

There was no public health service in Spain at this time so if you fell ill and could not afford to pay a doctor, you relied on folk wisdom and herbal treatments. Alcalá was well-known for the expertise of its *curanderas,* women with special healing powers. There was a small hospital, the Misericordia, built in the 16th century on the Plaza Alta. It was financed by the municipal charity board, and gradually fell into disrepair until it was demolished in the 1940s. There was also a hospice for elderly women at the Beaterio, which is still there today.

The Misericordia hospital, next to the old town hall

A report undertaken by two doctors in 1901 pointed out the poor health of alcalaínos at the lower end of the social scale. Workers and their families were permanently exhausted and hungry, living in unhygienic conditions:

Hygiene in this town is not as good as it should be, with a growing population, still lacking sewers in most streets; these are narrow and winding, the squares are few and small, the houses are low, small and most with no back yard, with many rooms below ground and shared with neighbours and animals …

A study on infant mortality rates in Alcalá between 1916 and 1921[16] showed that the town fared worse than the national average; a quarter of all deaths were in the first year of life. The main causes were perinatal infection, diarrhoea, enteritis, respiratory infection and malnutrition. The Ayuntamiento's attempts to improve public hygiene (some of them misguided, such as white-washing the public water sources in the belief that lime would kill bacteria) had not improved the condition of the most financially disadvantaged.

There was little help for mothers with sick children:

When your brother was just a year old he was struck with paralysis. I took him from the crib and he was like a skein of wool, floppy, unresponsive. I cried for help but nobody came … On top of that I was pregnant with you. I had no milk for him who needed it so much. I was desperate, I wanted to abort but couldn't – the potions I had taken didn't work. I resigned myself to my fate. Less than three years later your sister fell sick with typhus … the doctor tried everything but to no avail, she left us like a flower that never had a chance to bloom.

As for your brother, various doctors came and all said the same thing: there is no cure for paralysis. The last one we saw, in Cádiz, told us he would always be disabled but we could reduce the severity of his condition by bathing him for half an hour a day in warm water infused with basil, camomile, primula and lavender, then rubbing him down with camphor.[17]

At a national level there was growing awareness of the need to control epidemics of communicable diseases such as cholera, typhus and diphtheria. We can see evidence of this in the general public health measures outlined in the 1900 municipal byelaws quoted earlier. A compulsory smallpox vaccination programme was introduced in Alcalá in 1918.

Malaria was endemic in the region though within the town itself the Levante wind helped keep mosquitoes at bay. Between 1916 and 1921 a total of 23 deaths were attributed to malaria in Alcalá, nearly all of them campo workers during the spring and summer months. A study was commissioned in 1924 to investigate the causes, resulting in measures such as killing mosquito larvae in stagnant water with petrol, planting eucalyptus to help drain swampy ground, and doing away with open-air middens by regular burning or using the deposits as fertiliser. A mobile dispensary was used to distribute quinine to rural workers.[18]

There were no dentists. Problematic teeth would be extracted by barbers using a piece of string. There was no anaesthetic and after the extraction it was customary to adjourn to the nearest tavern and rinse well with a glass of wine.[6]

María Ulloa "La Partera", a professionally-trained midwife, arrived in Alcalá in the late 1920s and helped bring two generations of alcalaínos into the world. There is a street named after her near the Paseo.

Fairs and festivals

Fairs and festivals gave young men and women the chance to get to know each other, since there was little opportunity for socialising otherwise, especially for those who lived in the campo. The well-to-do would also hold parties in their private patios with the aim of finding suitable partners for their daughters. They were strictly chaperoned and not allowed to dance with their suitors; instead, the young man would offer a glass of sweet wine to the object of his attentions and sing her a little song.[6]

Feria

Alcaláinos enjoyed two fairs each year, the *feria de ganados* (livestock fair) in May, and the other in September coinciding with the *romería* (pilgrimage) to the Sanctuary a few miles away in honour of the town's patron, Nuestra Señora de los Santos.

Livestock fair

For the livestock fair the ganaderos brought their owners' animals to the Prado to sell. The meadows along the Barbate River thronged with cattle, oxen for ploughing, horses for riding or threshing, sheep for their fleeces, goats for milk and cheese, mules and donkeys for transport, pigs for breeding. The trading took place in the mornings and in the afternoon the men would go up to the Alameda to have a drink or two and buy items related to their trade – cowbells, tools, boots, saddles etc. - from the vendors' stalls. In the evening there was singing, dancing and other attractions on the Alameda and the Calle Real.

The September fair was held on the Alameda until the late 1920s, when it moved to the more spacious Paseo de Mochales (now called Paseo de la Playa). Naturally the owners of bars and shops around the Alameda were not happy about the move and petitioned the mayor to allow the fairs to occupy the Paseo in the daytime and the Alameda at night, but this was rejected.

Feria on the Alameda, 1927

Alcalá's bull-ring was completed in 1893, adjacent to the Paseo. It did not attract the biggest names in the business, but became well-known as a venue for young hopefuls (*maletillas*) to test their skill against calves and bullocks (*novillos*), usually bred in the area. These events coincided with the May and September fairs. It stopped being used for bullfights in the late 1920s, but the seating remained in place and public meetings and other events were held there. In later years it would become an open-air cinema and a discotheque.

Plaza de Toros

Carnival

Carnival, celebrated each year a few weeks before Easter, was an opportunity for residents to dress up in elaborate costumes, let their hair down, dance in the street and sing satirical songs mocking the latest fashions, public figures of the day, or their own neighbours. It had its origins in the festivities held before the deprivations of Lent, which have died out in much of the Christian world but survive spectacularly in places like New Orleans (Mardi Gras) and Rio de Janeiro. In the city and provincial towns of Cádiz they evolved into something very different:

> *In the 19th century singing took over from dancing as the main feature of Cádiz carnival. Performances were given by choirs on the street or in private homes. They wore costumes and sang a range of patriotic songs as well as* coplas *(popular songs), unaccompanied except for the beat of a drum. Later they began to accompany themselves with guitars and bandurrias. Over time the songs*

became more political and satirical, reflecting the voice of the working class. New World rhythms crept in, as the locals became influenced by the music and dance of the Caribbean sailors unloading cargo in the docks. Many working-class gaditanos had jobs on the ships between Cádiz and Havana.[19]

There were several distinct types of carnival group:

- *Chirigotas,* groups of six to ten men performing humorous songs about current topics. The songs were often introduced with kazoos, originally made from reeds.
- *Comparsas,* larger, more lyrical and more bitingly satirical than the chirigotas, featuring a dominant tenor voice.
- *Coros,* choirs of up to thirty members accompanied by an ensemble of guitars and bandurrias, with a repertoire that could be humorous or serious but often sang the praises of the city and its people.
- *Cuartetos,* small groups of comic street-performers, using two sticks for rhythm.
- *Romanceros,* solo storytellers using illustrations on an easel, which they pointed to with a stick while reciting.

Alcalá's carnival was notorious for its bawdy lyrics and wild behaviour. In 1918 the editor of the local newspaper, *El Castillo,* commented:

The God of Madness passed through the land leaving an indelible, unmistakable trail. In Alcalá a very sensible public notice was posted, which nobody complied with … the absurd comparsas were outstanding for their lack of ingenuity. The lyrics could not be more insulting, some-times immoral, and lacking all sense. Some children, fully tolerated by the authorities, sang obscene verses, incomprehensible on the lips of infants. In the end the Carnival was what it reasonably should be: a feast of corruption.[20]

Christmas

Christmas celebrations in Spain were low-key compared to other parts of the Christian world. There were no Christmas trees, cards or decorations. Instead families and businesses would each set up a miniature nativity scene called a *belén* (the Spanish name for Bethlehem). On Christmas Eve the family evening meal was followed by a mass (*misa de gallo*) to celebrate the birth of Christ. The lively folk-carols known as *villancicos* were sung during the mass and afterwards in the streets. Then things would return to normal until the night of 5th January, the eve of Epiphany, when the Three Kings (*Reyes Magos)* arrived unseen on their camels to leave gifts for the children. The Cabalgada, where the Magi ride through the streets during the evening distributing sweets, started to arrive in some of the larger cities during the 1920s.

San Jorge

St George had been Alcalá's patron saint since the 16th century, from which time every year on 23rd April the town would celebrate his saint's day with bull-runs, street-games and other festivities. However in 1900 the event was pared back to being a religious occasion, doing away with the release of bulls and instead distributing alms and bread to the poor. This continued until after the transition to democracy in the 1970s.

Religion and the Church

Alcalá had a number of religious brotherhoods (*hermandades* and *cofradias*) responsible for organising the elaborate and solemn processions during Semana Santa (Easter week), Corpus Christi and other events in the Catholic calendar. Each had their own (largely middle-class and male) membership and meeting-places, their own sculptures of Christ and the Virgin, and other imagery and equipment used in the processions. They also had a role in providing aid for the poor and mutual support for fellow members, not unlike the Freemasons.

There were three churches in the town:

- Parroquia de San Jorge, on the Plaza Alta (Plaza de San Jorge), constructed in the 16th century on the site of a mosque. In 1920 a new priest assigned to the town found it in a state of near ruin, and made an appeal to parishioners for funds to repair it.[21]
- Iglesia de San Francisco, commonly known as la Victoria, on the Alameda. This was damaged during the Lisbon earthquake and never properly repaired, and in 1887 it was closed due to the imminent danger of collapse. There was insufficient money in the municipal coffers to demolish and rebuild it. In 1903 it was declared safe again (the reason is unknown) and in 1909 work began on its restoration. It was inaugurated on New Year's Eve 1911, and a mass celebrated the following day.[22]
- Santo Domingo was part of a Dominican monastery located in what is now the cultural centre behind the covered market. It was closed during the 1920s and was later used as a school.

The Santuario de Nuestra Señora de los Santos is located a few miles outside the town on the site of the Battle of Vega de Pagana (1339) between the troops of King Alfonso XI and those of the Muslim leader Abu Malik. Before the battle the Christian soldiers were reportedly given a miraculous omen about the activities of the enemy, resulting in their victory. They erected a cross bearing the words "Sanctus, Sanctus, Sanctus" and a small temple was erected in honour of the Virgin. Some historians believe that the local name for the Virgin, Nuestra Señora de los Santos, derives from the words on the cross.

The building was extended and improved over the years and became a destination for pilgrims, especially on 12th September, the holy day of Alcalá's patroness, when alcalaínos of all social classes would make their way there on foot, horseback or wagon for the celebrations. In its chapel is one of the world's largest collections of votive offerings, little home-made drawings or paintings of sick or injured loved-ones to give thanks to the Virgin Mary for saving them.

St George, in the church that bears his name

La Victoria, in a state of disrepair

Santuario de Nuestra Señora de los Santos

Attitudes to the official Catholic church in Andalucía were ambiguous.[9] The upper and middle classes went to school and learned the received doctrine, as all schools were controlled by the church. Priests came from these classes, often the eldest sons. Attendance at mass and confession was a sign of class allegiance and conformity. A bad word from the priest could cost you your social status, even your job. Not only the middle classes but their direct employees had to attend. For women it was a chance to get out of the house and meet up with their friends.

The poor were mainly illiterate, the masses were held in Latin, and what little they knew about the Bible came from family or priests' readings. They rarely went to mass, being too busy with their families, living too far away and having nothing decent to wear. There was widespread anticlerical sentiment among the campesinos. They regarded the priests as idle and self-indulgent. Their beliefs were derived from the oral tradition and based largely on superstition; they believed in miracles, ghosts and the evil eye.

The Virgin Mary was their protector, and they petitioned her rather than pray directly to God. Many campesinos kept a small image of her in the home for this purpose. The Virgin was adored by working-class people in a way that the established Catholic Church eyed with some envy; she was a mother-figure, non-judgmental, she listened directly to their prayers without the need to go through an intermediary (priests were notorious for not respecting confidentiality in the confessional), and the celebrations in her honour were joyful rather than solemn. Jesus of Nazareth, displayed on the cross and paraded round the town during Easter week, was an object of pity. People were moved by his suffering, and women were especially drawn to the mother's tears.

Exvoto in the chapel of Nuestra Señora de los Santos

Jesús el Nazareno

Military Service and the Moroccan Wars

During the 18th and 19th centuries one in every five men aged 18 to 40 were randomly selected to join the Spanish army, a system known as *las Quintas*. Members of the aristocracy were exempt, and those who could afford it could pay for someone else to take their place. At the beginning of the 20th century the one-in-five rule was dropped and all men in this age group were theoretically eligible, but the wealthy could still opt out. From 1912 they were no more opt-outs but men were allowed to reduce the length of service considerably and choose which regiment they joined, on payment of of a fee of up to 5,000 pts (€20,000 in today's terms). This was well out of reach of the average working man.

Over half of the Spanish troops who fought in the Rif War in Morocco (1911-27), including many from Alcalá, were illiterate, from the poorest elements of society. Their training was minimal, their weapons often useless, contagious diseases (especially STDs) were rife and there were shortages of food and other essential supplies since corrupt officers were selling them on for profit. The death toll among Spanish troops was considerable.

In Alcalá the Ayuntamiento offered the services of its Misericordia hospital to treat the repatriated injured, and there were several fundraising efforts in the pueblo to help the families of the dead and wounded, including a bullfight. When the wars finally came to an end a stone plaque was erected by the entrance to the church on the Plaza Alta, dedicated to Alcalá's fallen. Very few of their bodies were ever repatriated.[23]

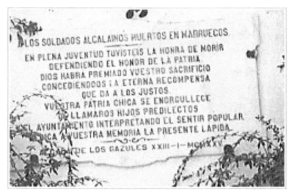

Commemorative plaque to Alcalá's victims in the Moroccan wars

CHAPTER 2 – 1931-1939

All wars are bad but Civil War is the worst of all, because it pits friend against friend, neighbour against neighbour, brother against brother. – Arturo Pérez-Reverte

Background

After the end of Primo de Rivera's dictatorship in 1930 a variety of factions including conservatives, socialists and Catalan nationalists joined forces to sign a pact with the aim of replacing the monarchy with a republic. The Bourbon king Alfonso XIII was deeply unpopular, and municipal elections held in April 1931 resulted in a landslide victory for the Republicans. The king went into exile and the Second Republic was declared. The electoral process was reformed in time for a general election in June, replacing single-member constituencies with party-based lists. Women could stand as candidates but could not yet vote. The result was a big victory for the Republican-Socialist coalition.

A new constitution came into force in December 1931. This established the rights to freedom of speech, freedom of association, women's suffrage and divorce. It stripped the nobility of any special legal status and attempted to disestablish the Catholic church, imposing strict controls on Church property, ending subsidies and banning religious orders from educating children. It set out procedures for nationalising public services, land, banks and railways. All Spain's regions had the right to autonomy. Spain had a new Republican flag, with red, yellow and purple bands, and a new national anthem.

The coalition quickly fell apart and in November 1933 a second election was held. It was won by the Spanish Confederation of the Autonomous Right (CEDA), led by José María Gil Robles, which capitalised on the increasing disenchantment among Catholics and conservatives. This was the first election in which women could vote. There had been some opposition to women's suffrage on the Left because of the fear that women were more likely to be influenced by the Church and vote for CEDA. There is certainly evidence that these six million new voters were heavily targeted by Gil Robles' party.[24]

Gil Robles formed a coalition with the Radical Republican party led by Alejandro Lerroux, which had also made a right turn. Under this administration there was significant social unrest as the working classes saw their hopes for a brighter future being systematically dismantled. The land reforms which would have made so much difference to the lives of alcalaínos were suspended along with most of the other reforms carried out under the previous government. This U-turn led in 1934 to a general strike and workers' rebellion in Asturias, during which miners occupied the capital Oviedo. It was brutally suppressed by General Francisco Franco and his Moroccan-trained troops; thousands were killed or taken prisoner, and reprisals against the rebels were savage.

By 1936 the coalition was collapsing. The Republican Radical Party was in open crisis as a result of the "Estraperlo" corruption scandal, in which party members had been bribed to lift a ban on roulette. Elections were called for 16 February, after the President had refused to allow Gil Robles to form a new government. The main parties of the Left formed an electoral coalition called the Popular Front, and those on the Right presented themselves as the Anti-revolutionary Front. The latter had great confidence that they would win, since their predictions excluded the potential vote for the Popular Front of the anarchist CNT members, who had abstained in the elections of 1933. However the Popular Front won with a small majority, both in the country and in Cádiz Province.

The progressive reforms planned by the Popular Front government were anathema to the wealthy landowners, the countless military generals left with idle hands following the end of the Moroccan wars, the Catholic Church, and the liberal and conservative politicians who had ruled without opposition under the *Turno Pacífico*. The reforms, they believed, could not be allowed to continue.

On 18th July 1936 there was a coup d'état, or "Glorious National Uprising" as the instigators called it, to rid the country of the twin evils of communism and anticlericalism. It had been carefully planned in advance by civilians, mainly members of the far-right minority movement *Falange Española de las Juntas de Ofensiva Nacional Sindicalista* (FE-JONS), supported by the Church and a substantial part of the military. Franco's troops were airlifted in from Morocco to help with the uprising (in planes supplied by Hitler) and he soon became leader of the movement.

The ensuing Civil War between the Republican government and the Nationalist insurgents lasted for just under three years. The Nationalists were assisted by their fascist allies in Italy and Germany. Hours after the outbreak of the war Adolf Hitler sent in powerful air and armoured units and used Spain as a testing ground for the Condor Legion, and Benito Mussolini supplied Italian warships, fighter planes, tanks, machine guns and 50,000 troops. Support for the Republicans came from the International Brigades (40,000 volunteers from 53 countries) and Mexico, who provided $2 million for rifles and cartridges as well as sanctuary for refugees. Other countries including the UK, France and the Soviet Union signed a Non-Intervention Agreement, though Stalin broke the agreement by covertly supplying aircraft, tanks and weapons, paid for with the Bank of Spain's gold reserves.

Spain's regular conscripts are estimated to have been evenly divided between the two sides, and both were joined by large numbers of volunteers at the outbreak of the war.

By July 1938 about two-thirds of the country was under Nationalist control. Although Madrid did not fall until the end of the war, the Republican government relocated first to Valencia and later to Barcelona, while Franco chose the northern city of Burgos as his seat of power. The Nationalists' superior firepower and support from their allies finally led to their victory on 1 April 1939, after the fall of first Barcelona and then Madrid.

The total death toll is contentious, with estimates ranging from 100,000 to two million.

Anarcho-syndicalism and the re-emergence of the CNT

The ideas of collectivist anarchism were based on the abolition of state, church and aristocracy, the three agents deemed responsible for the repression of the working class, and the development of free communities with spontaneous local justice and mutual support. They arrived in Spain in the late 19th century and quickly caught on among the freedom-loving but long-suffering campesinos of Andalucía.

By 1884 there were over 30,000 members of anarchist groups in Andalucía. The movement organised strikes and protests, notably among the vineyard workers around Jerez; the leaders were arrested and given long prison sentences, and by the end of the century numbers had dwindled to a mere handful.

Nonetheless this handful continued to evolve and organise. Random acts of rebellion by individuals gave way to carefully planned group action, with strikes, sabotage, demonstrations and boycotts. This form of revolutionary trade unionism was known as anarcho-syndicalism, and its ultimate aim was to overthrow the state via a general strike.[9]

The Confederación Nacional de Trabajo (CNT) had been founded in 1910 bringing together all the regional groups, and by 1919 it had over 700,000 members across the country. It was declared illegal under the dictatorship of Primo de Rivera, but re-emerged during the Second Republic. Its Alcalá branch was established in 1932 and one of the first to sign up was Juan Perales León:

The UGT opened a branch in Alcalá. I couldn't join because I was still too young. Then another centre opened, the CNT. They let me join. There people met and talked. The most knowledgeable of them were the organisers. What I wanted was a job, but perhaps because I wasn't old enough, they didn't give me work. Along with another youngster in the same situation, we wrote on the wall in the Calle Salá with bits of charcoal, in protest. We rebelled. It was my first act of rebellion.

… They formed us into Libertarian Youth groups so that we could develop awareness of what anarchism was. We managed to sign up those kids who were a bit special, who had a greater awareness, who were looking for something better. Anyone who got drunk, treated their family or girlfriend badly, or was always putting their foot in it, couldn't get in. We would not admit them. When someone wanted to join, we consulted each other. They called us the "eagle chicks of the FAI" .

Here in Alcalá there were six or seven Libertarian Youth groups and in each one there were eight young men, almost all of them working in the campo. Those who were better educated were the leaders, those who could read and write. Our mission was to prepare ourselves for the new society. We read many anarchist books and magazines. The CNT then was culturally very rich. The men were very well prepared. We had our library and went to the post office all the time to pick up books. Many books arrived. We educated and trained ourselves. To be a revolutionary was not just about firing shots and beating people up. We impregnated ourselves with pure anarchism. Although we couldn't put it into practice, it was what we wanted and we would fight for it. We thought we were the best, and the best ideas were ours. I still think that.

The Libertarian movement was very strong in Alcalá, Medina, Casas Viejas, Los Barrios, Jerez, Paterna, Jimena. We had contacts in all the towns. Sometimes there were strikes. They consisted of going out to the farms with sticks so that those who were working there would go on strike. When we came back the Guardia Civil would be waiting for us and would send us to jail. We were locked up many times, every time there was a strike. This happened during the Republic. Sometimes they beat us up. I remember one time when a guard, Molina, beat the shit out of your father on the Alameda.[25]

Although the anarchists rejected the established church as an instrument of repression, they were not necessarily atheists. As one of the Casas Viejas members put it:

Man, the sun, the sea are mysteries. I believe in a God who is above all things - who made the world, the sun, whatever you wish. But this God who puts people in hell and who talks to priests - him I don't believe in.[9]

They would however cite the life and death of Jesus Christ in their teachings to point out the hypocrisy of the state and the established church; killed by the capitalists, martyred by the priests, he was just another victim.

Some anarchists were vegetarian and teetotal, though neither was a requirement for membership. Alcohol and gambling led to conflict, so were considered a distraction from man's true calling, which was to improve himself and work in harmony with others. Bullfighting was considered barbaric, a remnant of medieval cruelty that desensitised people to suffering. Brothels were frowned on but mainly for reasons of hygiene (there was a high incidence of STDs and no antibiotics to treat them).

Illiteracy was a major issue because they believed men would never reach their true potential unless they could read. The CNT centres taught men to read and write, often using a literacy primer – the *Cartilla filológica española* – which workers would take away and study during their breaks. Guillermo García Jiménez, whose father was one of Alcalá's teacher-members, noted that the zeal to escape illiteracy was particularly strong in young alcalaínos, who could often be seen reading the works of philosopher Ortega y Gasset, Miguel de Unamuno, Emil Zola and Victor Hugo, or having heated debates on politics and philosophy in the bars.[6]

Some anarchists rejected the institution of marriage in favour of *amor libre*, free love, believing that men and women were equal and relationships should be based on mutual respect without the interference of church or state. Fidelity was fundamental in this respect; the association of "free love" with promiscuity didn't come along till the 1960s. However this was not common practice in Alcalá – if couples lived together without marrying (a third of children were born outside wedlock) it was most likely because they had no money for the fees. But infant mortality was extremely high, and rather than endure the stigma of having their babies buried in unconsecrated ground they would scrape together the money to have them baptised. Some more enlightened priests would do this for nothing.

Alcalá during the Second Republic

The 1931 Elections

As we saw in the previous chapter many alcalaínos lived in chronic poverty. The arrival of the Second Republic brought a real hope of improvement. Alcalá's first Republican mayor was sworn in on 5th June:

José Sandoval was a good man, worthy, and a believer who celebrated his appointment carrying two candles and covering himself with the mantle of the Virgin of the Saints. He was a man moderate in his political convictions, belonging to the middle class (his brother Manuel was editor of the weekly newspaper El Castillo de Alcalá, *and his other brother Francisco owned a bar). The family combined their liberal values with their religious beliefs, and in those first years of the Republic he was animated by a reformist spirit...*[6]

But he was a monarchist and a property owner, and regarded with suspicion by some.

REPÚBLICA ESPAÑOLA
1931

Shortly after the declaration of the Republic a law was introduced under which local people were to be given preference for any available employment. For Alcalá this should have meant the elimination of competition from cheap labour from Portugal and the Sierra de Málaga. There was also a requirement for landowners to hire a minimum number of workers depending on the extent of their cultivatable lands. But some landowners refused to comply, leading to tensions and culminating in a general strike organised by the CNT across the Province. The refusal to end the strike by a group of members from Medina Sidonia led to the Guardia Civil being brought in; two workers were shot to death and another five injured.[6]

The situation in Alcalá was further complicated by a fall in the price of wheat and cork, leading to reduced demand for workers. To alleviate the forced unemployment the Ayuntamiento requested funds from central government for public works, including the draining of part of the Laguna de la Janda and the distribution of the reclaimed land to tenant farmers who would provide work for jornaleros.

The CNT kept up the pressure for a reduction in the working day to six hours and a restriction on the introduction of new machinery. Neither side was willing to make concessions, more strikes were held and Sandoval stepped down in November 1931 due to ill health. His place was taken by Rodrigo Delgado Salas, who resigned for reasons unknown less than a year later.

The massacre at Casas Viejas

In January 1933 the Republican government was shaken to its foundations by the tragic events at Casas Viejas (now Benalup), just 20km from Alcalá. A small group of CNT militants trying to resist arrest, following a failed uprising in which one civil guard was killed and another injured, barricaded themselves inside a *choza* which was burned down with the men and their families still inside. Soldiers and guards then arrested everyone in the village who owned a gun, marched them to the site of the *choza* and shot them in the back. A total of 24 civilians were killed. It was never discovered whether the Prime Minister Manuel Azaña had given the order, but the events may have helped bring down his government.

When the news reached Alcalá local CNT members helped organise food supplies for those who had escaped the massacre and were hiding in the campo. To avoid suspicion they pretended to be harvesting wild asparagus. A week after the events one of them went to buy bread at the Venta de la Liebre, where the guards were waiting. They arrested and whipped him (a boy of 16) until he gave them the whereabouts of his colleagues, who were arrested and imprisoned in Medina Sidonia. When the trial arrived, on seeing the marks of the whips on their flesh the judge decided he could not hear evidence obtained by force, and set them free.

At the Alcalá carnival that year, the following verse was sung:

Casas Viejas, Casas Viejas,
Tus hijos piden reparto
Y el Gobierno por respuesta,
Te envia los Guardias de Asalto

(Casas Viejas, Casas Viejas, your sons asked for their share, and in response the government sent you the Assault Guards)[6]

Scene of the Casas Viejas massacre

Antonio Gallego Visglerio

Delgado Salas was replaced as mayor by Antonio Gallego Visglerio. Born in Alcalá in 1893, Gallego ran a bar and owned a lorry used to transport goods. He had been elected as a councillor for the Republican Socialists in 1931, and wrote a document outlining his hopes and plans on being elected to serve the Republic after many years of dictatorship and the collapse of the monarchy. He also described the difficult task that lay ahead for all the elected representatives - having to instigate investigations into corruption and wrongdoings of their predecessors, many of whom might be old friends or even family members. Not to do so, however, would be a betrayal of the people who had elected them.[26]

During May 1931 there were over a hundred incidents of anti-clerical Republicans setting fire to religious buildings across the country. Rumours reached the nuns at the Beaterio that men were coming from Cádiz to burn their premises. Gallego reassured them that "the people of Alcalá are noble and nobody is going to burn anything here. But if any of you are afraid, I offer you shelter in my house, which is big enough for everyone."[6] (He was right, there were no such arson attacks anywhere near the town.)

Gallego kick-started several projects to improve the town's amenities and create employment, but following CEDA's victory in November 1933 the Socialist administration was dismissed by the provincial governor and replaced with supporters of that party. He was reinstated as mayor, along with the rest of the elected council, following the Popular Front victory in 1936.

Public services and utilities

The covered market

In August 1931, under pressure from the builders' union, the Ayuntamiento commissioned a series of public works to address the unemployment crisis. One of these was the much-needed indoor market. Plans were drawn up with the hope of having it completed by 1935, but insufficient funds to purchase and demolish the derelict houses on the proposed site meant that the project was delayed and the Mercado de Abastos that now stands in Santo Domingo was not completed until January 1940.[27]

The public toilets

One small improvement for alcalaínos during this period was the construction of a public urinal on the Paseo de la República (now the Playa). It was built to an hexagonal design, reflecting the six urinals within, and finished with decorative brickwork. Unfortunately the level of cleaning was deficient, leading to protests from neighbours, many of whom thought such goings-on should be confined to the home. The objections came to a head when a charge was introduced to cover the cost of an attendant. A local builder offered to demolish it and replace it with an underground facility nearby, for use by women as well as men, beneath what later became the bar Siglo XXI. The project never came to fruition, due to the replacement of the socialist administration by CEDA following the 1934 election.[28]

Public conveniences on the Paseo

The football pitch on the Prado

Football was without doubt the most popular sport in Alcalá, but flat pieces of ground were hard to find and most games took place on the street. In February 1935 a resident asked the Ayuntamiento to prepare some ground on the Prado, the flat meadowland adjacent to the Barbate River, along with materials for goalposts so matches could be played there during the May fair. The proposal was approved unanimously. Seizing the opportunity, another resident asked permission to set up a stall next to the pitch to sell drinks, which was also approved. Football has been played on the Prado ever since.[29]

Education

Free education for all was a cornerstone of Republican policy. In August 1931 the Ayuntamiento unanimously agreed to build a new grade-school and requested funds from the Ministry of Public Instruction. It would have four classrooms, proper toilets, a library and offices for the staff. Early in 1932 the detailed proposal was submitted to the government for approval, where it seems to have languished in a drawer somewhere as the school was never built.

In 1933 the Ayuntamiento approached the Bishopric of Cádiz with a proposal to provide general education in the church within the Santo Domingo convent, which provided religious instruction, but this also failed to materialise as did a renewed attempt to build a school near the electricity works in 1935.[30]

The Popular Front government in Alcalá[31]

In Alcalá the leftist coalition won the February 1936 election with a greater margin than in the country as a whole, although less than a third of its 6,523 eligible citizens actually voted:

- Popular Front: 1,032 votes (55%)
- Anti-Revolutionary Front: 819 votes (45%)
- Falange: 33 votes

The tiny vote achieved by the Falange came despite a visit to Alcalá by its leader, José Antonio Primo de Rivera (son of the late dictator), a few days before the polls. He had been planning to address the town in the Gazul cinema (public meetings, rather than leaflets or canvassing, were the primary means of campaigning in those days). But a last-minute order from the Civil Governor in Cádiz forbade this, and instead he met with an intimate group of followers in private.

Victory for the Popular Front meant the return of many Republican and Socialist councillors who had formed the town's government after the 1931 elections only to be ousted two years later, including Antonio Gallego who was reinstated as mayor. The most pressing issues facing his new administration were enforced unemployment on the land, the cause of widespread poverty and hunger; a proper water supply for the town; universal free education independent from the Catholic church (one of the Republic's primary goals); and work on the second stage of the road to Jimena, for which a loan was needed.

Following standard practice at the time (known as *depuración*) Gallego's team began the purge from public office of those who were ideologically opposed to the Republican vision. This included several key members of the Falange and seven members of the Municipal Guard (including its chief, who would exact a bloody revenge in due course). Naturally there were complaints and protests, which fell on deaf ears, and public demonstrations were subsequently banned by the Provincial Governor.

Records from the municipal archive show the following key events during this short-lived administration:

- 9ᵗʰ March: telegram from the Civil Governor in Cádiz ordering surveillance posts on roads leading into the town, to watch out for "strange elements".
- 15ᵗʰ March: telegram from the Civil Governor banning public demonstrations.
- 15ᵗʰ March: arrest of the brothers Mariano, Julio and Pedro Toscano, landowners, for failure to hire workers at the agreed daily rate.
- 17ᵗʰ April: arrest of the former head of the Municipal Guard, José Tizón Jiménez.
- 2ⁿᵈ May: arrest of José Fernández Montes de Oca, member of the Falange.
- 6ᵗʰ May: designation of part of the estate of El Jautor (owned by the Toscano brothers) to be confiscated under the Agrarian Reform Act.
- 18ᵗʰ July: request from the Commander of Carabineros to come to Alcalá to organise a special surveillance service.

It is not hard to imagine the resentment and anger that was brewing among some of the more affluent inhabitants of Alcalá, indeed across the entire country. Their land, their wealth, the ease with which they could exploit a permanently hungry, illiterate labour force, and the brain-numbing indoctrination of the workers and their children by the Catholic church, were all under threat from the government of the Popular Front. The ground was fertile for the Falangists to spread their propaganda clandestinely, recruit new followers, stockpile arms, and collect financial donations for the "cause".

The Alcalá branch of the Falange was founded in February 1934 with the aid and encouragement of members from Medina Sidonia. Its leader was Miguel Blanco Sánchez (one of those arrested by the PF), with Ildefonso Marchante Romero as Secretary and Juan Armario Carrillo as Treasurer. Juan Armario took over as leader following Blanco's arrest, and at the beginning of July 1936 he received orders from higher up the chain of command to prepare for the National Uprising:

Copy of the order of the Movement to all local head-quarters in the Province of Cádiz (strictly confidential):

- All the local heads to whom this is directed must maintain the utmost secrecy about the points covered in it. Any indiscretion will be severely punished, as will any carelessness or lack of diligence to comply with its contents.

- At the same time as you receive these orders, the local head will give the necessary instructions so that all members are ready to mobilise at the first warning and willing to fulfil the tasks indicated to them.

- The local JONS will not intervene in the case of any military or civilian uprising, even if they have not received express orders from the provincial headquarters.

- The local head will have from this moment planned everything necessary for his transfer and that of the forces at his command, in cars or trucks, to the place indicated by HQ, taking the necessary steps to obtain the means of transport with all discretion and, naturally, without giving any kind of explanation.

You must acknowledge receipt of these instructions via the person who delivered them, using the attached sheet.

ARRIBA ESPAÑA!

The coup d'état of July 1936

On the morning of 18th July the final session of Antonio Gallego's council was held in the new Ayuntamiento on the Alameda, although he was away on an official visit to Seville. They dealt with routine matters - improved street-lighting on the Paseo de la República (now the Playa), justification of expenses for the mayor's trip to Cádiz, a payment of 20 pts for the coffin of "poor Miguel Jiménez", a payment to Jacinto Fernández for plumbing repairs, and a unanimous vote of condolence to the family of Señora Viuda de Silva on her death, "since the Municipal Corporation is grateful for her prompt collaboration on the many occasions when she was required to alleviate the unemployment of workers." There was no hint of the forthcoming tragedy.[32]

The following day the world turned upside down. The orders for the National Uprising had arrived, and within just a few days the Falangists were well and truly in charge. Their primary tactic to maintain control was to murder or imprison as many supporters of the Popular Front as possible and impose a rule of terror. There was no face-to-face fighting in Alcalá in the conventional sense of warfare, with two sides firing at each other from trenches; instead there was a prolonged guerrilla war in the montes and extrajudicial killings on the streets.

Reading the Falange diary one could imagine a relatively peaceful and short-lived takeover:[32]

> *19ᵗʰ July: ... the forces of the Falange are offered unconditionally to the Civil Guard and are beginning to serve under the command of the squadron leaders, patrolling the streets and being issued with weapons they have managed to collect ... In this way the glorious Falange Española is taking part in the glorious movement to save Spain – the Falangists are distributing themselves among the barracks of the Civil Guard and the fusiliers, and the rest are patrolling the streets.*

> *20ᵗʰ July: Now that war has been declared, the mayor and councillors are resisting handing over command. There are rumours going round that said mayor had sent messengers to those working on the cork harvest in nearby farms to come back and take over the town. But they were disarmed ... life in the town is as normal, the streets are seen to be very busy.*

A book describing the coup in Cádiz province from a Falangist perspective[33] noted that there was little or no organised resistance in Alcalá, where many able-bodied men were out of town working on the cork harvest:

On 19th July some people went to the military authorities asking them to declare a state of war, which they did straight away. From this date the town was patrolled by riflemen and distinguished supporters of the Falange, breaking up suspicious groups and establishing surveillance posts in strategic places to avoid disagreeable surprises from the Marxists of nearby towns.

The tranquillity was absolute, but on discovering that the authorities had sent messengers to the campo with the aim of getting certain elements to return to the town, the purpose of which we can easily guess, a group of Civil Guards and riflemen, along with some Falangists and others, went out to meet them and without resorting to violent means managed to disarm them, around four hundred, most of them armed with axes.

What actually happened was far from tranquil. On 19th July the Falangists marched down the Calle Real and took over the Town Hall by force. Guillermo Garcia Jiménez, still a child at the time, recalled:[6]

... I remember that young Manuel Venegas arrived at my parents' shop, completely shaken up ... He said: the señoritos have taken over the Ayuntamiento and are taking the axes off a team of corcheros returning to the town from the finca El Jautor. A group of Falangists are going down the Calle Real shouting "Viva España".

Juan Perales León, a member of the CNT, described that day in an interview with his nephew Carlos Perales:[27]

I lived in Calle Cádiz, and from my house I heard people talking about a demonstration. I set off down Calle Villabajo. My mother shouted at me not to go but I went anyway, believing that it was my own people. When I reached the post office I could see that a demonstration was coming through the Plazuela, but they were Falangists. They were shouting and carrying shotguns and rifles. It was a fascist demonstration ... They came through the Plazuela shouting out loud, with shotguns, rifles and all. In your house, where you live now, they had stored weapons, rifles, bullets and pistols in the well. One of those at the head of the demo was a doctor who they called Herrezuelo, who had treated me many times. I couldn't believe that he was a Falangist ... I was afraid they would catch me and arrest me. We knew it was an uprising, and that these people were armed, that they had come to rule over us, that they would come for us, and so it was."

The mayor, his deputy and the treasurer of the Popular Front administration were arrested on 21st July by Falangist troops and civil guards from Jerez. They were imprisoned in Medina Sidonia and executed by firing squad three days later, somewhere on the road between Paterna de Rivera and San José del Valle. The official reason for their execution was "*por no ser adicto al Movi- miento*" (for not being a supporter of the Movement). There are records of at least forty such executions, but the actual number of deaths is believed to be well over a hundred (José Tizón Jiménez, the sacked former chief of the Municipal Guard, was a particularly enthusiastic killer needing no other motive than revenge). Their belongings were confiscated and became the property of the new regime, and their wives and families were branded as Communists.

On 22nd July the council minutes register the takeover by the Falangists. The diary entry for that day reads:

Forces of the Falange and the Civil Guard effect the arrest of the Marxist mayor and councillors ... watch patrols are in place in the barracks and customs posts, a group of comrades make an exploratory journey to check the sites of Jautor and la Bovedilla, and another group make a discovery on the roads to Algeciras, Cádiz, Paterna and San José del Valle.

The cork harvest was in full swing and when news of the events reached the workers out in the montes, some of them went into hiding. Others, more trusting, returned to the town at the end of their shift only to face summary execution or imprisonment.

A battalion of civilian militia was organised, including a cavalry section, to raid farmhouses in the surrounding countryside, rounding up dissidents who were stealing grain and livestock and holding landowners to ransom. Others acted to monitor the public transport and postal services, search for arms caches, and report any subversive goings-on. They were extremely well organised and left nothing to chance:

> In those first few days a group of volunteers went out to a place known as Rocinejo, where according to rumours several Marxists were garrisoned. There was a strong exchange of fire which ended with the Reds running away, while our men recovered the livestock which they had stolen from various farmsteads. Also after a fierce struggle our men appropriated a thousand arrobas of charcoal which the Reds were keeping in a place called Montiforti. It was an excellent acquisition given that at that time there was an acute shortage of fuel.[33]

At the same time Falangist hitmen were murdering people with impunity during the night and leaving their bodies on the streets:

> The Civil War was already a reality across Spain, but even so the majority of people in Alcalá were trying to return to their day-to-day lives. Then the relative peace they had enjoyed for just a few short days began to collapse, as suddenly people from the town itself, fanatical supporters of the new regime, took up arms and with much hatred began what would be the most tragic period for Alcalá. They started the most atrocious and cruel repression anyone had known before then. My grandmother said that it was rare for morning to break without some dead body thrown onto the street.[34]

On 26th July a plane dropped a bomb on the town, killing and injuring several people including children in 91 Calle las Brozas. The Falangists maintained that this was an attempt by the Republican army to destroy their military headquarters; they fired at it from the ground and it flew off. They offered first-aid to the injured and one of their leaders, Juan Armario, drove them to hospital in Cádiz. But the word on the street was that it was a Nationalist plane, possibly Italian, which had intended to bomb Jimena or Ubrique (both still in the Republican zone) and hit Alcalá by mistake. According to Juan Perales León it was a common tactic of the fascists to force civilians to flee from the town so their homes could be looted. They regarded confiscation of goods as entirely legitimate. It was also fairly unlikely that the Republican army could have organised aerial responses so soon after the coup.

On 15th August the Falangists, the militia and the Guardia Civil celebrated a mass in the church of San Jorge, paraded through the streets to the Alameda bearing aloft the the red-and-yellow flag of the Nationalist movement, and ceremoniously hoisted it onto the town hall balcony, replacing the tricolour flag of the Republic. The ceremony was accompanied by triumphalist music and a salvo of shots.

A week later the new administration of Alcalá would be endorsed by the Civil Governor, with Juan Armario Carrillo, local head of the Falange, as mayor.

Civil War, Reprisals and Repression

From then on silence, slaughter and the encouragement of amnesia in the official version of events would be imposed on a generation of alcalaínos who lived through the cruel and pitiless torment of this massacre. In the council minutes of that same day you can read, among the routine actions of the new administration, of the release of 175 pts to the former mayor Antonio Gallego for his trips to Cádiz. His bones were still in a ditch somewhere, waiting to be unearthed.

... Repression, fear and blood became the normality which the people of the town were to experience for days, weeks, months, even years. Accusations, arrests and executions without trial brought dread to every house, every shadow of every tree, every street corner ... The walls of the cemetery were covered in blood, gunshots and bursts of shrapnel penetrated the ears and minds of the townspeople, provoking fear and terror. Trucks were crammed with men and women who, dragged from their homes, would end up as corpses in dispersed anonymous ditches ... They were people who never expected such a brutal repression on behalf of the forces marching under the banner of the National Movement. Many of the leaders most involved with the workers' cause had fled to the hills, and this saved their lives.[35]

The psychology of dehumanising the enemy had been practised for decades against the Arabs in North Africa and the same tactic was used against the Republicans, making it easier for soldiers to kill their former friends and neighbours without qualms of conscience by labelling them all as Marxist heathens, part of an atheist/communist threat to Spain's traditional values. General Gonzalo Queipo de Llano, commander of the Nationalist military forces in southern Spain, gave a speech to his troops on 23rd July 1936 via Radio Sevilla:

I authorise you to kill like a dog anyone who dares to resist you. If you have to do so, you will be exempt from any responsibility. ... Just impose the hardest punishment to silence those idiotic conspirators of Azaña. To this end I authorise all citizens who run into one of them to silence them with a shot. Or bring them to me, and I will shoot them myself.

*Our brave Legionnaires and Regulars have shown those
cowardly Reds what it means to be a man. And in
passing, the women as well. After all, these communists
and anarchists deserve it. Haven't they been playing
around with "free love"? Now at least they will now what
real men are, not military fags. They are not going to go
free, however much they struggle and kick.*

In August Queipo de Llano gave the order that all fugitives
were return to their home town for "security reasons". The army
and its volunteer supporters would take all necessary measures to
bring this about. Anyone not complying would be regarded as a
terrorist and punished. The *ley de fugas*, as it was known, was a
common means of extrajudicial execution. The killer had simply to
claim that his victim was attempting to resist arrest by running
away.

The Alcalá community was shattered. Neighbours denounced
neighbours, either out of spite or to put themselves in the good
books of the authorities. Spying and being spied on became a way
of life; you either fled and risked being hunted down, or stayed and
pretended to support the cause. The sierras of Aljibe became a
battleground, Alcalá's own front line where guerrillas and rebels
fought each other among the rocks and the cork-oaks.

*The social coexistence maintained throughout many years
between families and friends was dramatically broken in
the town ... it is certain that in that climate of terror, the
baseness of man came to light ... there were people
belonging to the lowest levels of Alcalá society who con-
verted themselves into executioners of the working class,
offering themselves as volunteers to shoot or beat up
many of their fellow companions of misfortune and weari-
ness. Groups of militia and Falangists started to prowl
the countryside around the town in order to hunt down
and capture Republicans and trades unionists.*[6]

The story of Ana Jiménez

As the official *Pacto de Olvido* (forgetting the past) began to lose its impact in the new millennium, many of the Alcalá victims' stories have been published by their descendants or by historians like Carlos Perales. This is one example, which illustrates all the elements of repression described above.[36]

> *Ana Jiménez was the mother of Joaquín García, schoolmaster and leader of the Republican Left, and the wife of Antonio García, leader of the local branch of the CNT. After the coup her husband and Joaquín, fearing the atrocious repression which was beginning to take place in Alcalá, went into hiding for several months in the hills to the east of the town.*

> *Ana and her younger son Guillermo went to stay with friends at a mill in Patriste. From time to time she returned to Alcalá to pick up supplies from her grocery shop in Calle los Pozos. On 15th August she was arrested and interrogated about the whereabouts of her husband and son.*

> *Many years later her neighbour Juana told Guillermo that she went to visit her in prison (located in Las Monjas off the Plaza Alta) and found her in a bad way, so bad that the wife of Diego the jailer, a good woman, had prepared her an infusion of some sort. The next day Juana went back to the prison to take her something for breakfast but she was no longer there. Early that morning she had left the prison and it was not known in which direction she had been taken. She would never return. Many others would have taken the same route from the prison, down Calle Cádiz towards Calle Diego Centeno, where some sinister lorry would pick them up and take them to their death.*

Her story is one that had a major impact on the town, not least because she was a woman whose only misdemeanour was to be the wife and mother of men with progressive ideas. As a reprisal, because they had fled, she was murdered.

The long years of silence produced many rumours in the town. Some claimed she had been denounced for having a Republican flag in her house; others suggested that she was betrayed by a builder who owed money at the shop. Today such a motive seems incredible, but in those months and years of savage repression, anything could happen.

As if her murder wasn't punishment enough, her house and shop were looted. Many neighbours remember a lorry at the door, loading up goods. Others said that they had subsequently seen some of the goods in other people's houses, including that of a workman who had joined the rebels and whose betrayals sent many Alcalá idealists to face the firing squad. It wouldn't be the first such case, and it wouldn't be the last.

José María Franco Rodríguez

An example of *depuración* (purging) is graphically illustrated by the case of José María Franco Rodríguez.[37] A native of Algar and a doctor by profession, he had held the office of Auditor in Alcalá for two years when the coup occurred. He was arrested with the mayor and other elected representatives and taken to the prison in Medina Sidonia. His belongings were immediately confiscated. Someone was seen riding his precious white horse a few days later, and his typewriter was spotted in a neighbour's house. Apart from belonging to the Popular Front, there is no evidence that he had committed any misdemeanour.

His stay in the Medina prison lasted rather longer than his colleagues'. He suffered psychological torture at the hands of his jailers, who called on him to confess and mocked him with the taunt "now it's your turn" on a regular basis. When he was finally executed some time in September, he was so thin and weak he had to sit in a chair. He left a wife and a fifteen-year-old daughter.

Francisco Pizarro Torres

The total number of alcalaínos who died during the coup and the subsequent reprisals is not known, but estimates range from 50 to 400. No mass graves have been found in the pueblo; it appears that they were taken elsewhere to be disposed of. Jerome Mintz in his studies on Benalup-Casas Viejas was told by one of his interviewees that many alcalaínos were buried around that town. We know that Francisco Pizarro Torres was one of them, from the account related by his sister Francisca to her granddaughter:[34]

On her return [to Alcalá from the prison in La Línea] *she discovered that her brother Francisco was being held in custody. They wouldn't let her see him. The jailer took pity on my grandmother with everything she had gone through, and told her to come back in the morning when he would let her in. One morning she was told he was no longer there. The same answer must have been heard by many other families of execution victims. They had taken him the previous night to Casas Viejas.*

There were witnesses to his execution, most notably a woman who lived nearby and saw how they shot him in the legs, leaving him badly injured. This woman said that when he asked for water he was told to go to the river. This he did, dragging himself along, finally managing to reach the river where he bled to death.

Francisca herself was captured and imprisoned along with her baby daughter for refusing to give the whereabouts of her husband, another CNT member, but subsequently released following the intervention of her brother José's employer, a member of the Falange.

The taking of La Sauceda

La Sauceda was a village of around 2,000 people about 20km north-east of Alcalá as the vulture flies, in the mountains between Puerto de Galiz and Jimena de la Frontera. Life was hard, a constant struggle against the climate, wolves and foxes, and the rocky terrain with little cultivable land. The villagers were tough and resilient. Following the coup it was a natural destination for leftist refugees from Alcalá and other towns in the area, and the population increased by several hundred.

The first attempt by the Nationalists to take over La Sauceda, shortly after the coup, involved 300 Moroccan troops and some civilians including Falange supporters from Alcalá. The villagers fought them back with shotguns and stones, and after a week or so they retreated. Stronger measures would be needed to obliterate this centre of resistance.

On 30th October planes from the German Condor Legion wiped the village off the map. It was the first systematic aerial bombardment of civilians, preceding the better-known Guernica attack by six months. The following day four military columns marched in. They rounded up the remaining villagers and either shot them on the spot or took them to the nearby Cortijo de Marrufo, where they were held and tortured for months before being executed and their bodies dumped in communal graves.[38]

In 2012 work began on excavating and reburying the bodies. Only 28 were found, of which 13 were identified through DNA testing. The actual death toll was more like 600.

You can visit La Sauceda today and rent one of the restored stone cottages for an escapist adventure in the Alcornocales Natural Park. No electricity, no wifi, but plenty of ghosts.

Remains of the church at La Sauceda, bombed by the Condor Legion

Alcalaínos in the Civil War

Military service was compulsory in Spain and many of those who were serving in the armed forces at the time of the uprising found themselves fighting for the Nationalists against the government. Some deserted and went to the Republican zone to fight the fascists, as did some of those being persecuted by the new regime. This left a severe shortage of able-bodied men in the town. In September 1937 the Republican magazine *La Libertad* published a report from an Alcalá man who had been imprisoned for desertion in Cartagena:

> *In my battalion there were many soldiers from my town ... they told me what had been happening there ... at least 145 people had been shot for supposedly being involved in anti-fascist movements. Those who were not shot were at the Front. Hardly any crops had been sown, and what little there was was being harvested by women and old men.[39]*

After the end of the war in 1939 Franco created the National Service for the Placement of Ex-combatants and Ex-captives, and the mayor was required to complete a census. From this document we know that there were 550 Alcalá men fighting for the Nationalists, equating to more than 20% of men of working age. It does not include those who died in battle, nor those who fought on the Republican side either as registered militia or as volunteers.[40]

Membership of the Falange in Alcalá

For anyone holding any kind of salaried post in either the public or private sector, or running a business, joining the Falange was obligatory. In Alcalá around three hundred people applied for membership in the months following the coup, including some agricultural labourers. There is no way of knowing whether they genuinely supported the Nationalist cause or just wanted to avoid persecution and feed their families.

At the beginning of 1936 the town's population was around 9,500. In the February 1936 general election there were only 33 votes for the Falange. Documents in the municipal archive show the rapid growth of the party following the coup:

- Fifteen civilian members were actively involved in the July uprising, working alongside the civil guards and the militia.
- Three months later there were 81 members, each contributing 30 pts a month.
- By June 1937 nearly a thousand inhabitants were in some way affiliated to the party, according to data compiled by the local head of the Falange:
  - 135 members of the *Primera Línea* (civilians actively involved in acts of violence)
  - 109 members of the *Segunda Línea*
  - 67 "sympathisers"
  - 184 *Flechas* (under-18s)
  - 89 members of the *Sección Femenina*
  - 65 female *Flechas*
  - 12 female sympathisers
  - 328 members of the CNS, then the only legal trade union. (Former UGT members were automatically enrolled in the CNS so were not necessarily supporters of the Falange.)

Sección Femenina

Founded by Pilar Primo de Rivera, sister of José Antonio, the women's section of the Falange was required to set an example of domestic womanhood in line with the party's ideals: patriotic, devoutly Catholic and subordinate to men in every way. Pilar summed up the organization's mission as *"a silent, constant labour that will bring us no compensation other than thinking how, thanks to the Falange, women will be cleaner, children will be healthier and houses will be tidier"*. Women were discouraged from having minds of their own or developing any creative talent, but assisted with the distribution of aid to the deserving poor under the *Auxilio Social* programme, and organised sporting events, folk-dancing and the like.

Members of the *Sección Femenina* were also required to report regularly on any neighbours showing signs of deviation from the path of righteousness. Correspondence in the municipal archive indicates that the women of Alcalá were somewhat negligent in this respect, occasionally being reprimanded by the Provincial Head for failing to submit their monthly observations.

The Church

All attempts made during the Second Republic to reduce the influence of the Catholic church were immediately revoked by the Falange. Civil marriages were declared invalid, divorce and contraception became illegal, children could only be given the names of Christian saints, and priests were given the same powers for policing the population as local government officials and Falangist leaders. Attendance at religious ceremonies in the Catholic calendar was obligatory for senior party members, who had to wear their official Falange uniform, and attendance at mass was wise move for everyone else.

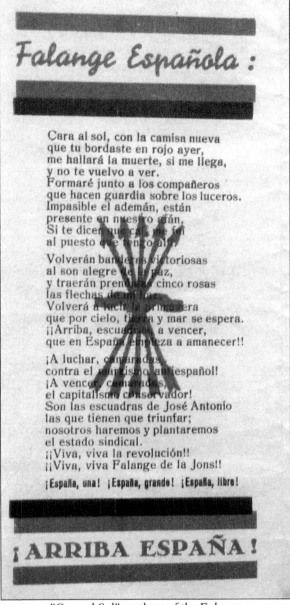

"Cara al Sol", anthem of the Falange

CHAPTER 3 – 1940-1960

We have torn up Marxist materialism and we have dis-
orientated Masonry. We have thwarted the Satanic
machinations of the clandestine Masonic super-state,
despite its control of the world's press and numerous
international politicians. Spain's struggle is a Crusade;
as soldiers of God we carry with us the evangelism of the
world! (Francisco Franco, 1945)

Background

With Francisco Franco as its leader (*Caudillo*), supported by the security forces and the Catholic church, Spain remained under an authoritarian dictatorship during the whole of this period. The purges and reprisals against supporters of the Republic continued well after the end of the Civil War, and people's everyday lives were observed and controlled to an extraordinary degree.

Although Spain was officially neutral during the Second World War Franco helped his former allies in various ways, including sending 18,000 volunteers to assist Hitler in fighting the Russians on the Eastern front. Because they couldn't wear the official Spanish army uniform they wore the blue shirts of the Falangists, and were thus known as the División Azul (Blue Division).

After the end of the Civil War Spain remained isolated from the rest of the world in a self-declared autarky (economic self-sufficiency) and suffered a chronic economic depression. But once the Cold War started Franco's anti-Communist stance made him a natural ally of the USA. In 1953 the two countries signed the Pact of Madrid, which resulted in the US supplying substantial financial assistance in return of the right to develop and use military bases on Spanish soil, including the one at Rota on the Cádiz coast. At the same time reforms were made to end Spain's economic isolation. The United Nations quietly dropped its condemnation of the fascist regime and allowed Spain to join in 1955. In 1958 it was given access to loans from the IMF and the World Bank, which funded the "Spanish Miracle" described in the next chapter.

Law of Political Responsibilities

The persecution of the opposition did not end once the Civil War was over. The Law of Political Responsibilities came into force on 13th February 1939, targeting all supporters of the Second Spanish Republic and former members of leftist parties. It was retroactive, dating back to October 1934, which meant that anyone following the decrees of the elected Republican government was criminalised for "assisting rebellion". If found guilty, they (or their families if they were dead or missing) could be fined and their assets confiscated. Further penalties included the restriction of professional activities, limitation of freedom of residence, and even forfeiture of Spanish citizenship.[41]

Enforcing this law involved highly intrusive intervention into people's personal lives, and much report-writing. This led to a massive amount of paperwork, and Alcalá's municipal archive contains literally thousands of related documents. Everyone occupying professional posts had to swear a written declaration of allegiance to the Movement, including personal details of themselves and their parents, what they were doing on 18th July 1936, any previous political or trade union affiliation (including Freemasonry, of which Franco had a passionate hatred), details of what they did to assist in the Uprising (supplying arms or vehicles, serving on surveillance posts etc.), and names of witnesses who could corroborate their declaration. In addition the Provincial government, military commanders and numerous other regional and national bodies required the head of the local Falange to provide detailed reports on personal conduct and beliefs for everyone holding public office, including teachers, medics and members of the various security forces. Transfers to posts in other towns required a good conduct report from the mayor. All forms of communication, postal and telephonic, were censored.

The law was nominally repealed in 1945, after half a million people had been subjected to it.

"The Hunger Years"

During the 1940s the country suffered chronic food shortages, and Andalucía was especially hard hit. The decade began with a severe drought that lasted for three years. Large numbers of agricultural workers had been killed, injured, imprisoned or gone into exile during the Civil War, and less than 10% of land in the municipality of Alcalá was under cultivation.

Alcalá's main food-crop, wheat, was appropriated by the government via the *Servicio Nacional de Trigo*, with landowners and millers kept under strict observation. Nonetheless a flourishing black market developed, which benefited the big landowners most as they were less likely to be kept under close scrutiny. Some local millers managed to hide the odd sack of flour from the inspectors and smuggle it home for their families and neighbours. Mothers fed their children on *gachas*, a mixture of flour, oil and sugar cooked up with a pinch of cinnamon for flavour. They could conceal a pocketful of stolen flour more easily than a loaf.

Rationing was introduced in 1939 but was nutritionally insufficient: weekly rations consisted of 125g of meat, 100g rice, 100g lentils, one egg, a piece of soap, and 250g of "black" bread (made from non-wheat flour such as maize, chickpeas or carob, sometimes bulked out with sawdust). Ex-combatants who had fought on the Nationalist side in the Civil War received an extra 250g of bread, and priests and members of the Guardia Civil were allowed 350g of white bread.[42] Only widows of men who had died fighting for the Nationalists received pensions. There was no help for those on the losing side unless they were deemed worthy of assistance under the programme known as the *Auxilio Social*.

Often there were insufficient supplies to distribute even these minimal rations. People resorted to stealing food to feed their families, scouring the countryside for edible plants and snails, trapping wild birds, or buying goods on the black market if they could afford it. On Fridays the poor were allowed to ask for coins or bread from their more fortunate neighbours; it was not unusual to see queues of women, children and the elderly outside the doorways on the Calle Real.

The black market

The black market thrived during this period of shortages. It had three forms, all lucrative but high-risk. Several alcalaínos made a small fortune during the 1940s; others lost their lives.

Contrabandistas sold scarce luxuries such as coffee, penicillin or American tobacco smuggled in from Gibraltar or picked up somewhere on the Cádiz coast. They travelled in teams at night to avoid the Guardia Civil, hiding their strings of horses during the day, sometimes passing through Alcalá on their way from the coast to towns in the Sierra.

Estraperlistas sold essential goods produced in Spain such as flour, sugar or olive oil that had escaped the eye of the government inspectors (often in return for a share of the profits), bypassing the rationing system.

Mochileros went into Gibraltar and purchased goods legally which they then brought back over the border in a suitcase to sell at higher prices. Women who did this, known as *matuteras*, took the bus to La Linea and walked across the border, occasionally entering the British colony with slender figures and returning a few hours later, apparently heavily pregnant.

Groups of men would keep a covert eye on the black marketeers' comings and goings, sitting around chatting at strategic positions on the roads into the pueblo. The wooden hut near the top of the cycle lane built in 2010 replaced one of these unofficial observation posts; it was affectionately known as "La Moncloa" (the seat of government in Madrid).

Resistance, prison or exile: the fate of Republicans after the war

Fugitives who had fled the town during the coup continued to live under cover in the montes and the campo after the war ended. Some of them joined organised resistance groups known as the *maquis*, after the French Resistance fighters in WW2, although to the fascists they were merely *bandoleros* (bandits) to be shot on sight if caught. The terms *maquis* and *guerrilla* were banned by the regime in 1947.[43] They survived by stealing produce and livestock from farms, occasionally kidnapping members of the farmers' families and using the ransom money to buy supplies. There were fifteen such kidnappings recorded in Alcalá. This led many small and medium-sized landowners to move with their families to the safety of the pueblo.

In 1949 the *maquis* convened a meeting in the Sierra de Cabra, the mountain range to the north-east of Alcalá. They created the Fermin Galán group, with about thirty members, vowing to continue their organised resistance. Their secret headquarters were based near Medina Sidonia. One of the members was known as Pedro de Alcalá. He escaped an attack on the camp by the Guardia Civil in December 1949 (one of their colleagues had betrayed the group in return for a pardon). He and the other survivors, barefoot and with no warm clothes, made their way to the mountains to fight for another year until were killed by the Guardia Civil near Cortes de la Frontera after a tip-off from a farmer.[44]

Some alcalaínos who had spent the war in the Republican zone returned to Alcalá after the war and turned themselves in. They were tried and imprisoned, but pressure on the prison system plus a shortage of manpower on the land led to a system of parole known as *libertad condicional,* where they were obliged to remain in their home town and report to the authorities regularly.

A maquis group near Medina Sidonia

Hundreds of thousands of political prisoners were sent to forced-labour camps. There were 55 such camps in Andalucía alone. Sometimes the men were joined by their families, and lived in shacks they built themselves after their shift was over. There was no schooling or other luxuries for the children.

One of the biggest was Los Marinales near Dos Hermanas in Seville, which opened in 1940 and did not close until 1962. Ten thousand men dug a canal across the Guadalquivir basin, 150 km long, with no earth-moving equipment. Some of the roads out of Alcalá, such as those leading to Puerto de Galiz and Patriste, were built with slave labour during this time.

Slave labour at Los Marinales

Some Republican supporters fled across the Pyrenees to France, only to be incarcerated in the concentration camp on the beach at Argelès-sur-Mer. When WW2 broke out many of them fought alongside the French Resistance against the Nazis. An Alcalá man, José Mora Gómez, was one of 4,427 Spanish Republicans who lost their lives in the Mauthauzen concentration camp in Austria.[45] Others left Europe for the Americas, following in the footsteps of the Alcalá socialists who escaped persecution by settling in Argentina in the late 19th century. Some never returned, others came home as old men after the end of the dictatorship.

Guillermo García's brother Joaquín remained in Buenos Aires until 1989, and died a few weeks after his return to Alcalá.

Earning a living from the montes

During the 1940s campesinos started to arrive in Alcalá from near and far to take advantage of the demand for products of the montes, working on their own account rather than putting themselves up for hire. They built unregulated dwellings in settlements on the outskirts of the town – San Antonio, Monte Ortega, Calle Altillo, Pozo Abajo. Some were little more than shacks with a patch of land to grow food, but others were extended and improved over the years.

Charcoal production was the main attraction, much in demand due to the shortage of other kinds of fuel. Many families set themselves up as carboneros, putting pressure on the sustainability of the forest and occasionally coming into conflict with people who had lived and worked here all their lives.

Carboneros building their oven

But charcoal could only be made in the winter months. At other times of the year the campo offered a variety of alternative income sources, including harvesting edible plants such as *tagarninas* (golden thistle), wild asparagus, prickly pears, figs, palm hearts, oregano and thyme, and selling them from door to door. Also profitable during spring and early summer was the collection of medicinal plants such as *poleo* (pennyroyal, a cure-all for everything from period pains to bronchitis), *zaragatona* (psyllium, a powerful laxative) and *mostaza* (white mustard, a diuretic thought to prevent infection). The plants were sold to the pharmacist, who would boil them down to extract essential oils.

Families with their own h*uertas* (orchards and vegetable gardens) sold their surplus produce. These were usually the responsibility of women, who as well as working in the home might also raise poultry and a pig or two, selling eggs and produce to customers calling at the *huerta:* oranges, plums, quinces, pomegranates, pears, radishes, onions, tomatoes, cabbages and cauliflowers. They might also sell direct to the teams working in the campo, or take the produce into the town to sell.

Hunting and poaching also brought in revenue for those in possession of a shotgun or handy with a snare. Birds and rabbits caught eating newly-sown crops could legally be shot. Licensed hunting went into decline during and after the War, due to strict gun control and the guerrilla war between the *maquis* and the Guardia Civil. This allowed the populations of wild boar and fallow deer to recover, offering lucrative opportunities for poachers who could sell the meat at the rural stores/eating places known as *ventas*. The author Luis Berenguer befriended one such poacher on his many visits to Alcalá, buying him a new shotgun after his own was confiscated by the Guardia Civil. Berenguer wrote about his exploits and narrow escapes from the authorities in a best-selling book, *El Mundo de Juan Lobón.* In 1989 it was turned into a TV series, somewhat less faithful to reality than the book.[6]

Reminiscences

We can learn much about life in Alcalá in the middle decades of the 20th century from the written accounts of those who lived through them.

Juan Leiva, who grew up here during the 1940s, related his childhood memories in a book[7] which although somewhat sentimental in parts does give us an insight into this dark period:

> *I was about eight years old. It was the postwar era, those years of famine, the 1940s. Alcalá at that time had around 12,000 inhabitants. But many people died, especially children, and many young men never came back from the war. The ravages of hunger showed no mercy to the weak. The basic foodstuffs were in short supply. People made a fortune from contraband and the black market. Earnings from wild asparagus, tagarninas and poached game were the salvation of many families. Others were forced to emigrate.*

As an altar-boy at the church on the Alameda, he recalls the frequent funerals he had to attend:

> *We put on our red cassocks, white surplices and coloured capes, and Father Manuel wore a black cassock, white surplice, stole and black cape. Manolo carried the sprinkler and a bowl of holy water, and I carried the incense burner. We waited in the doorway of La Victoria. Soon we saw a procession coming down Calle Los Pozos. A man was carrying in his arms a white coffin, no more than a metre long, accompanied by a group of neighbours. He was weeping and calling out the child's name. The crowd accompanied him in complete silence. Women did not attend funerals, they stayed at home accompanied by female neighbours and prayed. It was a paradoxical image to see a man of the land, strong and tough, crying like a child, with a white coffin in his arms.*

From that day on I noticed that children's funerals were very common. Some children died at birth, others of hunger, the rest from tuberculosis. Treatment with penicillin, discovered by Alexander Fleming in 1929, had not yet reached Spain. The children's funerals surprised me, because I couldn't work out how a child could die of hunger or TB or how a man could cry.

Leiva's family was reasonably well-off and did not suffer the worst deprivations of the era, as the following extracts show:

Alcalá's home-baked sweets and pastries were excellent; cakes made with olive oil, almond cakes, raisin cakes, "angel hair" cakes, meringues, marzipan ... the latter was one of Juan Ramos's specialities. He made elaborate little marzipan figurines and sold them to the children in the streets .... They were playful figures of animals and real-life characters from Alcalá. The fried sweets were equally exquisite; doughnuts, honeyed fritters, fried bread or picatostes, leche frita, fried pastry rings, cinnamon buns made by a gipsy who had a stall on the Alameda ... And the sweets made at Christmas and Easter: rice pudding; pumpkin in honey from the mountains; stuffed cheese with honey; quince in syrup ...

In the middle of December all the families began their preparations for Christmas. Those who were able to had slaughtered a pig, so there was no shortage of chorizo, black pudding, crackling, chitterlings and salami during the festive period. The smell of Alcalá's traditional pork products impregnated every corner of the town. The splendid sausages were put by in the store-rooms and lofts of the houses to be cured ready for Christmas Eve and Christmas Day.

The Alameda

At the centre of my memories of Alcalá is "La Alameda de la Cruz", where the main streets of the town met. In the early morning sure-footed muleteers and day-workers could be seen leaving, refreshed after a night's sleep. They returned at dusk after working all day. They cleaned themselves up and met in the bars, or sat in the doorways chatting. The square took on an amazing vitality from eight to eleven at night. After dinner the women sat on the pavements outside their houses discussing the topic of the day ... The young men went to the Calle Real to watch the girls go by. The bells in the tower of San Jorge emitted sonorous chimes for the evening service, which hung in the air like a host of angels clothed in moonlight. The bells in the Victoria belfry had a more metallic sound, scaring the pigeons from the vault and jangling all round the square.

The Alameda

The smells of the square were unmistakable. From Vicente's bar came the scent of coffee and anise; from the hunters' club, sherry wines and game from the shoot;

from Dominguito's, marinated offal; from the pub, sea-food and beer; from the bakers' bar, fried songbirds... Each bar had its speciality. In those days wine from Chiclana and tapas from Alcalá were favourites, good and cheap. The men would say that for five pesetas you could feed yourself and get tipsy.

The children of the town would gather there almost all year round. We played the same games as always; catch, skipping, hopscotch, marbles, football, leapfrog, until our mothers had to call us in for dinner...

Francisco Teodoro Sánchez Vera was born in 1945, left Alcalá to study, found work in Catalonia and never returned on a permanent basis, but regularly contributes to the town's annual review *Apuntes Históricos*. Here he describes his childhood in the 1950s:[46]

My first memories relate to our new house in Calle los Pozos ... I see myself on a little tricycle with a wooden seat, pedalling around the legs of the dining table, or going up the steep street with a little wicker chair under my arm on the way to school. I remember the streets cobbled with stones from the River Barbate, and the pavements of unequally-sized slabs to make walking more comfortable ... I also remember the beauty of the railings and balconies, the numerous courtyards packed with large families, and the charming little alleys. It was a lively and busy street with people and horses continually passing through. My world was my street. I played endlessly with my friends and spent the best part of the day there, the night as well when spring and the long summer arrived. The neighbours brought chairs out onto the pavements and chatted in the fresh air, while we children carried on with our games. It was the same in more or less all the streets in the town.

There was still no television in Spain. It didn't reach Andalucía until the end of the decade, and people com-

municated with each other much more than they do now. The doors of the houses were always open. The common entertainment was the radio. Everyone listened to the midday news, the serials, the romantic soap operas which caused so much controversy among their listeners, the sentimental songs, the football results, and at 10 p.m. the prizewinning lottery number for the day.

Artist and sculptor **Manuel Jiménez Vargas-Machuca** lived in Alcalá as a child in the 1950s. He clearly had a vivid imagination from an early age:[47]

We waited miserably for the rain to clear up so that we could go out and take over the street again. While waiting I thought about the "sacamanteca" men – I never understood that. Is it possible that there were human beings who dedicated themselves to extracting the blood of children so they could sell it later? Did these men not have children? How could they possibly kill a little child who had never harmed anyone?

Apparently these fearful beings came from "beyond the compass", or behind the "Lario". They were places where children of our age could not go alone. How scary! They terrified us with those stories. We were also told that in some houses of the Lario there were ghosts. They wore white sheets and moved without feet, as if flying through the air...

Francisco (Paco) Pizarro Medina was born in 1936, the third of seven children, and described his childhood in his autobiography.[48] His father José was a baker, and his mother collected firewood.

The family home in Calle Rio Verde consisted of just one room and a cooking area under the stairs. So José borrowed the money from his boss to buy a further room upstairs, which is where we children slept.

Work in the bakery was long and hard. José had to get up in the small hours to make the dough, light the wood-fired oven, cook the bread, and then load the loaves onto mules to sell them round the streets. So eventually he decided to open a bar. It was christened "Los Panaderos" and was located on the Alameda next to the church. It served whatever foods were easily available – tagarninas, wild asparagus and artichokes in spring, the meat from the matanza (pig-slaughter) over the winter, barbel, carp and eels during the fishing season.

When I was seven I felt obliged to start contributing to the family's finances. After school I collected cigarette ends from the streets and bars: a tinful would earn 50 cents. The woman who bought them would roll them up into fresh cigarettes, making five or six from a tinful.

My next job, at the age of eight, was selling newspapers door-to-door and on the street. My father didn't approve of this sort of child labour, but eventually gave his consent. I did well, not only selling all the papers that were delivered but receiving small gifts from my customers, such as milk, cakes and fruit. In the evenings I sold sweets at the local cinema, which meant I got to see the films. I was particularly impressed by Marlene Dietrich and Humphrey Bogart. I also made toys for Christmas presents, such as brightly coloured hoops made out of old bicycle wheels.

Once the Panaderos bar was up and running I gave up my other jobs, going there after school to clean fish and fry sardines. I left school at 12 and went to work there full time. A teacher, Don Antonio, believed I had artistic and dramatic talents and offered to pay for me to continue my education, but my father refused as he needed me to work in the bar...

Paco lost his virginity in a brothel on the Plaza Alta, to a prostitute named "Ana la Gorda". He and his friends weren't officially allowed in because they were under 21, but the madam said they could come in the afternoon when there were no other customers. The five of them lined up and took her one after the other, and then had to clean themselves with potassium permanganate solution to avoid infection.

Public services and utilities

The monumental task of financing and constructing a proper water supply for Alcalá, which had preoccupied successive administrations for decades, finally came to fruition early in the 1950s. It was owned and administered by the Ayuntamiento, as is still the case today.

In 1950 the owner of the electricity company died and there was a proposal to take it into public ownership. The mayor argued:

It is a well-known fact that the private sector turns its back on business related to the provision of public services, seeking more productive investments where the intervention of the administration is less intense. Specifically in relation to the supply of electricity to small towns ... thus we find that the electricity service of Alcalá de los Gazules is in the hands of a private company which acquires and resells current from Seville, does not fully cover the needs of our people, and fails to make the improvements necessary to meet our growing requirements ... that could only be achieved in the hands of the Ayuntamiento, whose aim is not to make a quick profit but the well-being and prosperity of the population.[49]

A price was agreed and a loan applied for, to be repaid from the sale of electricity. However the Local Credit Bank in Madrid, having looked at the books, decided that Alcalá would not be able to repay this additional loan on top of what they had already borrowed to finance the water supply. It was eventually sold to a private buyer.

The familiar orange *bombonas*, butane gas cylinders for domestic use, first arrived in Spain in 1957 but did not reach Alcalá until several years later; charcoal continued to be the main fuel for cooking during the period covered by this chapter.

Education

At the beginning of this period the only options for schooling were the Beaterio on the Plaza Alta, run by nuns (by the 1940s they accepted boys as well as girls), or a handful of teachers who gave classes for a fee, sometimes in their own homes. The largest was that of Manuel Marchante, whom we met in Chapter 1:

> *Don Manuel was a widower, he had two sons, he always wore black and he was old. The school had just one class for forty or fifty children ranging from 5 to 12 years old, and the older ones taught the smallest ones to read. The classroom was situated in an alley which led down from the Calle Real to the Rio Verde. It was shaped like an L, and the furniture consisted of a crucifix, the teacher's table and chair, a large blackboard, some maps on the walls and a cupboard for the books. He always wore glasses with big thick lenses for his myopia. In the morning the classes were orderly and we made good use of the time. But in the afternoon Don Manuel would come back from lunch somewhat drowsy, which sometimes caused him to nod off ... then chaos would reign.*[7]

In 1946 the mayor Juan Armario Carrillo revisited the idea of a purpose-built school in Alcalá and set about obtaining land and funding. Work on the new school, located at the end of Calle los Pozos, did not commence until 1953 and it opened two years later with five classrooms for boys and two for girls. The sexes also had separate playgrounds and entrances. In December 1954 it was decided to name the school after Juan Armario, who had died a few days before.[30]

The Juan Armario school

The *Escuelas Profesionales de la Sagrada Familia* (SAFA) is a Jesuit institution founded in Burgos in 1940 to give free basic education and vocational training to youngsters from poor families. In 1955 it opened a school in Alcalá in a restored building formerly owned by the Franciscan community near the Plaza Alta. Initially it offered 160 places for boys and girls aged between 8 and 11; the upper age limit was subsequently raised to 14.

Patio of the Sagrada Familia school (SAFA)

For those who lived outside the pueblo and had no way of getting to school, itinerant teachers were hired to teach reading, writing and arithmetic to the children of the middle-classes in their own homes. They usually lacked any formal qualification, and some had been sacked from their previous posts for one reason or another. They worked for board and lodging plus a modest fee, often having to travel miles on foot, bicycle or horseback from one client to the next.

Towards the end of the 1950s a number of rural schools were set up by the Provincial education department for the children of campesinos. They remained in place until the end of the 1960s. The teachers came from as far afield as the Canary Islands and Galicia, and were nearly all women. A few men taught adult literacy, but it wasn't thought appropriate that they should teach young girls, especially when the subjects included domestic chores.

Rocinejo rural school

The schoolmistresses were not very keen on going to these remote rural schools, so the posts were mainly taken by newly qualified teachers on their first post, often just 19 or 20 and living away from home for the first time, not used to campo life with no electricity or running

water and having to pee in a tin or go behind the stables.
They usually had to share a bedroom, sometimes even a
bed, with the children or grandmother in the house where
they were staying. They didn't have a choice, they had to
earn a living and pay back what their parents had
invested in their education. But some looked back on it as
a positive experience, and developed close relationships
with the families that put them up.[50]

Cinema

Cinema was a major form of escapism from the hardships and narrow horizons of daily life, both for adults and for children. As well as the Cine Gazul, built in 1928, several more came and went during the period covered in this chapter. The open-air Cine España was located in the former bullring on the Paseo. In its first year (1946) the screen was destroyed by the Levante, so after that they improvised with a folding screen which could be hoisted on pulleys. It was in competition with the Cine Avenida, where Pizarro's restaurant now stands, and there were fierce price wars. The Cine España closed in 1950 and the equipment was purchased by José María Sánchez, who used it to open the Cine Maravillas on the site now occupied by La Cabaña. That closed in 1960, unable to compete with the more luxurious and better-equipped Cine Andalucía in Santo Domingo, which opened in 1957.[51]

The regime took full advantage of the big screen to spread its propaganda, particularly relating to religion and the military. Franco himself co-wrote the script for *Raza* (Race), whose IMDB entry reads:

When the Spanish Republic is declared in 1931, three
brothers go their separate ways. One, a priest, is killed by
leftists. One, a member of the government, betrays his
family's traditional ideals. The third fights on the side of
Franco to defend them.

The films were accompanied by NO-DO newsreels (*Noticiarios y Documentales*) produced by the State, which had a monopoly on public information.

The censors applied four levels of suitability: Suitable for Children (PVM), Can be Seen (PV), Tolerable (T) and Morally Reprehensible (MR). When American films started to arrive they were heavily edited and dubbed into Spanish to avoid any risk of moral or political corruption. Any depiction of divorce, adultery, sensuality, revealing clothing or incitement to public disorder was unacceptable. Posters were altered to hide women's legs and cleavage, bedroom scenes were cut altogether, and even Donald Duck did not escape the scissors: one scene where he raised his fist in the air was cut because it was reminiscent of a Communist salute.[52]

A few alcalaínos had long-wave radio sets and listened clandestinely to the BBC or the Voice of America during WW2, as Radio España only ever reported international events that were favourable to the fascists. Gonzalo's barber-shop on Calle Real was a favourite place for disseminating what was actually happening in the world.[6]

Football

Another escape route from the drudgery of daily life was Spain's favourite sport. Franco used it to promote Nationalist values and provide a safety valve for pent-up discontent:

> *The Spaniard was not permitted to think, still less spread ideas which were not in keeping with the fundamental principles of the Movement, but was allowed once a week to go to a crowded enclosed space and give vent to all his anxieties and frustrations ... by yelling insults at the referee or the opposition.*[6]

Franco chose Real Madrid to represent the "true" values of Spain, financing the construction of a new stadium and investing in top players so that they would win international trophies and improve the country's reputation abroad. It paid off, for in the 1950s they won five consecutive European Cups.

At home, he used the club's traditional rivalry with Barcelona as a way of punishing the rebellious Catalans. In the semi-final of the 1943 Copa del Generalísmo, Barcelona won the first leg 3-1 at home. Before the second leg one of Franco's officials paid a visit to the Barcelona players, ominously reminding them that they were only allowed to play because of the generosity of the Caudillo. They walked out onto the pitch for the second leg to blood-curdling screams and whistles from the hostile crowd. Fans behind the goal hurled abuse and physical objects at the Barça goalkeeper, forcing him to leave the penalty box for much of the game. The referee turned a blind eye and Madrid won 11-1.[53]

In Alcalá, kicking a ball about was a favourite occupation for children:

And so we went out into the street and managed to improvise a football pitch. Our footballs were just paper or rags tied up with string, which might last the whole afternoon. Now and again someone got hold of a rubber ball; that was a real luxury. The problem with our football pitches was the steep hills. If one of those rubber balls rolled away, we had to run like the devil after it. Sometimes the balls would go up on the roof. We had to devise ingenious ways of retrieving our precious treasure - with broomsticks or the rods used to pick the prickly pears, or by climbing on top of each other – otherwise the ball would stay on the roof and our game would be over for the day. But we were very happy.[47]

The official town side played for a while in *"el hoyo de la Fábrica"*, a large hole in the ground left after excavations for the electricity factory, where the municipal park is today:

It consisted of an enormous pit, twenty or thirty metres deep. The bottom had been flattened out to make a football pitch. There the Alcalá team played against other teams from the area. On match days the whole town would come down to the Playa to watch the game … [7]

Football in "el Hoyo"

Fairs and festivals

The main events continued to be the livestock fair in May and the Romería in September. In 1949 the present system of auctioning rooms at the Santuario during the Romería celebrations was introduced. Instead of being restricted to members of the Brotherhood, they were allocated to those who donated the largest amounts of money (in sealed envelopes).[54]

The familiar carnival celebrations with their satirical songs were banned under the Falangist regime and replaced by "Traditional Festivals of Cádiz", where the entertainment was bland and heavily censored. Nonetheless the *carnavalistas* carried on writing and singing their verses in secret, in out-of-the-way places away from the watchful eye of the authorities.

St John's Eve, 23rd - 24th June, marked the summer solstice. Youngsters gathered wood from the fields and bits of old furniture to build a huge bonfire on the Plaza Alta. When night fell they tied pots and pans to a rope and towed them through the streets leading up to the square, while blowing horns and ringing bells. At midnight they lit the fire and danced around it, or jumped over it if they wanted to impress the crowd.

On Christmas Eve (*nochebuena*) the celebration of Midnight Mass after the family meal was one of the biggest events of the year, and the church was always packed. Afterwards the young people took out bottles of anise and brandy and went through the streets singing *villancicos,* accompanied by the drumming of spoons on the anise bottles, and asking the neighbours for cakes and sweets.

St George's Day (23rd April) was still just a one-day event at this time, with few diversions other than religious ceremonies.

Día de la Raza (12th October) celebrated the arrival of Christopher Columbus in the Americas, which marked the beginning of Spain's imperial conquests. It was a public holiday and schoolchildren had to learn the colours of the different "races" - white, black, yellow, red - paint their faces and don appropriate costumes in order to parade through the streets. Many of the children took their pets with them, as they had seen images of Columbus with parrots on his shoulder or in cages when he returned to be presented to the Catholic Kings. There were no parrots in Alcalá, so they improvised with lesser kestrels and pigeons.[55]

Feria 1947

Petitioning the Virgin to make it rain, 1949

Romería in the 1950s

CHAPTER 4 – 1961-1978

Leave me, when I die, in my corner of Andalucía
so my body might fertilise its soil.
Leave me next to the Cross,
embracing the roots of the leafy olive trees
which I contemplated with such happiness
on my visits to Los Santos,
when I was among the living.
Leave me to fly freely over the whitewashed houses,
over the red-brown cork-oaks,
over the Playa with no sea.
Leave me to sleep in the arms of my beloved Holy Mother.

- Francisco Teodoro Sánchez Vera, economic migrant

Background

Between 1959 and 1974 Spain experienced an economic boom known as the "Spanish Miracle". It was initiated by a team of modernising technocrats appointed by Franco, most of whom were members of the Catholic cult Opus Dei. Their development plans, financed with loans from the IMF, gave Spain the second highest growth rate in the world (behind Japan), reinvigorating the old industrial zones in the Basque Country, Catalonia and the area around Madrid. A state-disciplined labour force with no interference from unions over pay or working conditions made Spain especially attractive to investors from the USA, France and Germany. There was massive investment in state-owned industries such as the SEAT car plant in Barcelona, shipbuilding, steelworks and petrochemicals.

There was very little industrial development in southern Spain, and the principal effect of the "miracle" in Andalucía was large-scale depopulation as people moved north to find work. But another strand to Franco's process of modernisation was the development of mass tourism. Under the management of Manuel Fraga, Minister of Information and Tourism from 1962 to 1969, Spain opened up its pristine Mediterranean coastline to sun-seeking holiday-makers by building hotels and apartment blocks, creating employment opportunities in the construction and hospitality industries.

Franco abolished entry visas for tourists and devalued the peseta to make it cheaper to visit, and Europe relaxed the regulations on charter flights for package holidays. The number of foreign visitors rose from under two million a year in the late 1950s to 18 million in 1967 and 30 million in 1975. The first to take advantage of low-budget tourism were the Scandinavians, soon followed by the British. Fraga marketed the country with the slogan "Spain is different". It certainly was; few of those visitors were aware they were holidaying in a fascist dictatorship. But they brought much-needed hard currency, and helped broaden the horizons of the Spanish people with their free and easy lifestyle, '60s clothes and pop music.

Following Franco's death in November 1975 his chosen successor Juan Carlos Bourbon was installed as monarch, swearing allegiance to the principles of the "Glorious National Movement", and the bureaucratic infrastructure of the Francoist regime remained in place. Depending on one's point of view, the new King either skilfully guided Spain towards a modern constitutional democracy or reluctantly conceded to pressure from home and abroad to put an end to its single-party authoritarianism.

The initial plan, based on gradual reform of the institutions in place during the dictatorship, was drawn up by Francoists Carlos Aria and Manuel Fraga. It collapsed in June 1976, failing to satisfy either the demands of the far right or those of the regime's opponents on the left.

The King then appointed another of Franco's former ministers, Adolfo Suárez, as Prime Minister charged with bringing about the transition to democracy as quickly as possible. Suárez decriminal-ised membership of trades unions and opposition parties, including Basque and Catalan separatists and the Communist Party (PCE). He dissolved Franco's secret police and replaced some of the most extreme military hardliners with moderates. He declared an amnesty for political prisoners, and an unwritten guarantee of immunity from prosecution for crimes committed during the civil war and the dictatorship. This policy of closing the door on the past was known as the *Pacto de Olvido*, the pact of forgetting.

The Law for Political Reform was approved by the Cortes and backed by 94% of voters in a referendum in December 1976, paving the way for a general election in June 1977. Suárez's party, the UCD, received 35% of votes compared to 29% for the PSOE and 9% for the PCE.

A new Constitution, the result of many months of argument and compromise, established Spain as a democracy subject to the rule of law, enshrining human rights and stressing the values of liberty, justice, equality and political pluralism. It also repealed all pre-existing laws that contradicted these rights. In a national referendum on 6th December 1978 it was approved by 92% of voters (the turnout was 67%). This date remains a public holiday, *Día de la Constitución*.

Life in Alcalá

In 1967 the Bishop of Cádiz, lamenting the effects of *latifundismo* on the Province (which at that time had one of the highest unemployment rates in the country), wrote:

> *More and more fincas dedicated to the easy exploitation of livestock, where few hands are employed and there is no need to worry about social issues ... Continuing to live in the campo is considered, even by the campesinos themselves, as showing a lack of courage, a sign of human decadence... the dwellings are often deficient, the diet repetitive, primitive and scarce. They pine for a drop of running water in the house, and in many cases for electric light. The school is far away and hard to get to, going out for any form of entertainment is almost unheard of. They either lack completely or have great difficulty in accessing medical care ... in these conditions, who would not think of leaving?[5]*

In 1960 the population of Alcalá was 11,221, the highest ever recorded. Ten years later it had fallen to 7,519, and by 1980 it was down to 5,879. The reasons behind Alcalá's dramatic depopulation relate largely to changes in the town's traditional sources of employment – agriculture, livestock and the forests of the montes.

Agriculture

Increased mechanisation and the introduction of monoculture crops such as sugar-beet, which could easily be harvested by machine, significantly reduced the demand for labour on arable land. Tractors replaced oxen for ploughing and sowing, combine harvesters replaced reapers, and aerial herbicide sprays replaced the women and children employed for weeding (and also killed some of the wild plants traditionally foraged for food). The last of Alcalá's many flour-mills closed in the mid-1970s, made redundant by larger industrial complexes outside the town.

Agricultural workers' daily rates had quadrupled between 1952 and 1963. The rancheros who could not afford to buy tractors or pay higher wages sold up and left, and the latifundistas, no longer obliged to grow food crops for the government, switched to breeding fighting bulls which needed less investment and manpower. One of the biggest such estates in Alcalá was Ahijón, owned by the Domecq family who had made their fortune in sherry.

By the late 1960s there was very little crop cultivation left in Alcalá. Casual workers had to travel outside the area to Medina, Benalup, San José del Valle or Arcos, where intensive cultivation of industrial crops such as cotton and sugar-beet was taking place as a result of the technocrats' development plans.

The estate which attracted the greatest number of alcalaíno workers was Las Lomas, between Benalup and Vejer. It was owned by the Marquis of Tamarón, José Ramón Mora Figueroa, who was keen to employ the most modern farming methods to exploit the recently-drained lagoon of La Janda. He housed 200 families on the estate, with brick-built houses, shops, a cinema, a school and medical services.

> *However the fortunate employees had to pay a price in terms of loss of their liberty. The estate was completely fenced in, and visitors had to register with an armed guard at the gate. Everyone was watched at all times. If a tractor was damaged, the worker driving it was fined. Workers were expected to attend Mass every Sunday and Doña Carmen* [the Marquis's wife] *would do unannounced home inspections to make sure they were clean and tidy. They were not allowed to raise chickens or grow anything but flowers, and they were fined if they dropped litter. This was all too much for some workers, as was the sight of women labouring in the fields.*[19]

Unfortunately Mora's zeal for progress did not extend to how he treated his seasonal workers. One woman from Alcalá described how a group of them walked to Las Lomas carrying all their belongings at the beginning of January to work the cotton season.

They slept in unheated, overcrowded, flea-infested barns and had to light candles to dry the dew off the cotton before they could pick it.[5]

The Marquis was a close friend of Franco, who invested heavily in the development of Las Lomas. When the Generalísimo came down to hunt on the estate, the workers were taken to a bridge and made to line up and salute him, watching hungrily as lorries laden with venison and partridges rolled by.

Workers' cottages at Las Lomas

Livestock

During the 1950s an epidemic of African swine fever had all but wiped out the Iberian pigs which had grazed freely amongst the oak trees of the *dehesas*. The hardy and adaptable *retinta* cattle were introduced in the 1960s; unlike the fighting bulls, they could graze on rough ground in the montes, but fences had to be built to retain them and they had to be fattened on alfalfa or hay before going to market. This created work, but their profitability later suffered from cheap Argentinian beef imports. The demand for oxen for ploughing had all but disappeared by this time, and the use of horses, mules and donkeys for transport was in decline.

In the early 1970s fast-growing pines and eucalyptus were planted in the *montes propios* as cash-crops, and anyone whose animals were caught eating the saplings was fined. When the rancheros tried to rent grazing land they found themselves in competition with the hunting lobby, who wanted to fatten up their deer. For many that was the last straw. Some sold up and moved away. Others moved into the pueblo and just used their land in the campo to grow food for their own families. The number of small farms (less than 1.5 hectares) in the municipal district of Alcalá fell from 247 in 1952 to just 56 thirty years later; the beneficiaries were the large estates.

Retinta cattle in the montes

The Montes

The arrival of other forms of fuel for cooking and heating led to the virtual disappearance of charcoal production and the collection of firewood, both significant for the town's economy. Ironically once the carboneros had gone the trails and forest floor became so overgrown that the landowners had to pay men to clear the undergrowth before the cork harvest – often the same men who had paid the landowners for the right to do this in the past.

However there was one new source of income for campesinos wanting to work on their own account: digging up the bulbous roots of tree-heath (Erica arborea) and taking them to a new factory which was set up in the town. There they were trimmed and baked, then sent to Barcelona, London or New York to be made into briar pipes for smoking tobacco. This was an important business in Alcalá for a few years but no pipes were ever made locally, and the processing factory closed around 1970.

In 1971 management of Alcalá's woodland passed to a government agency, ICONA, charged with replacing old and damaged cork-oaks, planting new species, creating and maintaining fire-breaks, and promoting the increasingly lucrative hunting industry. The *maquis* were no longer a threat, and owners of estates in the montes restocked their land with red deer for weekend hunting parties, leaving armed guards in charge during the week to deter poachers.

New contractual jobs were created by ICONA's projects but it also removed one of the last remaining rights of people working for themselves, that of collecting wood to make tools and furniture; growing demand from outside the area meant they had to pay market rates.[5]

Employment within the pueblo

The gradual increase in living standards meant that many small businesses prospered. The increase in car ownership led to a growing demand for mechanics and dealers. More people could afford new clothes and shoes, or the occasional meal out. José Pizarro did so well at his new bar next to the bus-stop, La Parada, that he was able to buy the site of the old open-air cinema on the

Paseo and build what is now the Restaurante Pizarro. Pepe Perales expanded his haberdashery business on the Calle Real, Tejidos Perales, to sell other goods; he also opened a warehouse on the Alameda selling mattresses, a shoe-shop on Rio Verde, and a store in Benalup:

> *It wasn't just haberdashery. Rolls of oilcloth of all colours were piled on one of the balconies. Shirts, lots of them, multicoloured, ordered by size piled up in their respective boxes on the side of the counter. IKE was the best-selling brand. Terylene trousers, blazers - Lois was the brand name then. Countless rolls of fabric were piled on the counter, of all sizes, colours and qualities; ribbons, zips, socks, briefs, panties, bras, jackets, sweaters, raincoats, sheets, blankets... You had to jump over the counter to serve the customers. There was a trap-door but it was always shut because of the stuff piled on top of it...[56]*

Other trades went into decline, especially those associated with traditional agricultural equipment, or repairing items that people could now afford to replace.

Working away from home

The revival of industrial activities in other parts of Spain, recruitment programmes from manufacturing industries abroad (especially Germany, Switzerland and France) looking for cheap labour, and the development of the Costa del Sol for mass tourism all offered well-paid jobs for those prepared to leave their home town. Between 1964 and 1973 an average 4,000 workers a year from Cádiz province went abroad to work, and similar numbers went to other Spanish regions. The 1973 international oil crisis brought this migration pattern to an end, and several alcalaínos drove home in Mercedes-Benz cars which they had helped to make.

The boom in construction work on the coasts of Cádiz and Málaga provinces provided high wages for both skilled tradesmen and labourers. Sometimes they would be away from home for months at a time, sleeping rough in the buildings they were working on, and sending money home to their families. Some would stay away during the week and come home on Saturday afternoon to spend Sunday with the family, returning on Monday on the early morning bus. Others would make a permanent move, putting down new roots in the hope of better opportunities for their children.

Once the tourist industry was established on the Costa del Sol younger men and women from Alcalá found work in related businesses such as hotels, restaurants, beauty salons or laundries. The distance was too far to commute, and wages did not usually stretch to car ownership, so they rented flats close to their work. Once settled they sometimes arranged for their parents and siblings to come and live nearby.

In the 1970s it became common to see dozens of Alcalá women waiting for the bus early on Monday morning on their way to Cádiz, Seville or Algeciras to work as domestic servants in the homes of well-to-do city-dwellers. The writer Fernando Quiñones became particularly fond of one of them, who used to turn up for work at the start of the week with a bunch of fresh greens, a rabbit or some good Alcalá bread.[5]

Community Employment Programme

In 1971 the government set up the *Empleo Comunitario* scheme (EC) to provide work for agricultural workers during the long periods of forced unemployment. Each Ayuntamiento could apply for funds to offer contracts of not more than three months a year at 75% of the national minimum wage. The work had to be of benefit to the community and could be carried out anywhere within the municipality, both the town itself and its public lands. The scheme provided relief for many families, but also helped dissipate any growing dissatisfaction that might lead to organised protest, and acted as an indirect subsidy to employers.

In order to apply for work under the scheme men had to prove their jornalero status by presenting an official card stamped by the employers to indicate they had been paid the agreed daily rate. The cards were not issued to women, even though they had been labouring alongside the men in the fields for years (for half the pay). If their husband died or became unable to do heavy physical work, they had no recourse to any form of government assistance.[57]

In December 1971 the Ayuntamiento received the sum of 1,600,000 pts (worth €200,738 in 2020) which was used to plant eucalyptus on the Coracha to prevent soil erosion, repair the road surface of Calle Nuestra Señora de los Santos, and carry out other minor works in the pueblo.

In subsequent years EC funds were used to help finance the cork harvest on fincas owned by the municipality. Because the most skilled corcheros could find better-paid work with the teams working on private estates, this led to a deterioration in the quality of the work and irreparable damage was done to many trees.

Corcheros

Housing

As more and more campesinos left the land and moved into the pueblo, and standards of acceptable hygiene rose steadily, Alcalá experienced a growing shortage of habitable dwellings for the working class. Following inspections by Jesuit priests who found worrying levels of homelessness amongst the poor, the Brotherhood of Our Lady of the Saints built a total of forty-two houses in the town. In 1967 the final twelve were blessed by the Bishop of Cádiz, who laid the first stone.[58]

In 1968 a law was passed promoting the building of social housing (*Viviendas de Protección Pública*, or VPOs) to be sold or rented to local people at below market value on condition that they did not resell them for profit. There were two categories: Group I was for those with a reliable income who could obtain a mortgage from the *Caja de Ahorro* (savings bank), and Group II, aimed at those on lower incomes and more heavily subsidised. The blocks of flats on the old Finca de los Larios, on the side of a hill to the south of the town, were early examples of Group I VPOs. Unfortunately it was not deemed necessary to include lifts.

Public services and utilities

Between 1968 and 1973 the town's electricity supply was substantially improved by replacing the decaying wooden posts that carried the cables from Alcalá to the generator in Medina Sidonia.

This provided a back-up supply if the local generator failed, and permitted the extension of electricity to peripheral settlements such as Pozo Abajo and Patriste.[9]

Bottled butane gas replaced charcoal as the primary means of heating and cooking during the 1960s, though charcoal-burning braziers placed under a circular table were keeping the feet of alcalaínos warm in winter well into the 21st century. In the early days the bright orange gas bottles, known as *bombonas*, were delivered by donkey-cart.

Inter-urban roads were improved to cope with growing amounts of traffic, including the road to Benalup which was paved in 1969. A number of private bus companies offered services to other towns in the province and to Seville.

In 1960 there were six hundred new cars registered in the Province of Cádiz; by 1975 the annual total had risen to just under ten thousand. The SEAT 600 was mass-produced in Barcelona via a joint venture between the Spanish government, six banks and the Italian car-producer Fiat. It was affordable on easy repayment terms, changing the lives of many alcalaínos with regular jobs, though carts drawn by mules or donkeys were still widely used in the campo.

SEAT 600, The People's Car

The first "bombonas"

Alcalá's first fire engine, c. 1970

Education

A law passed in 1953 had established a requirement for secondary education culminating in a *bachillerato* (an exam-based diploma). Ten years later the Alcalá government decided it was time for the town to have its own secondary school, as the only ways students could achieve this qualification were to move elsewhere or have private tuition at home. At first they proposed incorporating it into SAFA, the Jesuit school which had opened in 1955, but SAFA only wanted to offer a diploma in agriculture taught via evening classes.

The Ayuntamiento therefore decided to take on the project itself and spent the next few years applying for funds, commissioning plans and getting approval from various bodies. Building work started in March 1967 on a new school with 320 places and a maximum monthly inscription of 200 pts (€27 at 2020 values). It was named after Pedro Sainz de Andino, an alcalaíno who wrote Spain's first commercial trade rulebook in 1829.[59]

In 1969 new industrial zones including steelworks and oil refineries were set up on the Campo de Gibraltar and the Bay of Cádiz, in attempt to mitigate unemployment and the adverse effects of the closure of the border with Gibraltar. SAFA with its professionally-trained staff offered scholarships for vocational diplomas in different kinds of engineering, not only for alcalaínos but people from other towns in the district. Students often did their initial studies in Alcalá and then went to the larger SAFA college in Úbeda (Jaén) to complete their training.

Fairs and festivals

Feria

The spring fair gradually became less relevant for the buying and selling of livestock, but was still celebrated in the mid-1970s, as the poster below shows. It was held in June and featured events such as clay-pigeon shooting and a motor-bike gymkhana.

The September fair in honour of Nuestra Señora de los Santos featured similar attractions as well as concerts, dances, cock-racing, a beauty contest, football matches, horseback parades and the usual fairground attractions such as tombola and bumper-cars. It kicked off at 8 a.m. with a *diana floreada,* a military-style reveille played by a marching band.[60]

Family picnic at the Sanctuary

The ferias and and the festivities at the Sanctuary of the Virgin provided an insight into the social structure of Alcalá:

The Caseta Municipal, located in the park, was a place where agricultural labourers did not go until the arrival of democracy. It served as a meeting place for local sectors linked to the regime - livestock breeders, council workers, businessmen, students and schoolteachers. A brick wall, in place until quite recently, separated them from the rest of the locals. The majority of rancheros and tenant farmers could access this area but preferred not to, and sat at the tables and chairs in the other bars and chiringuitos on the Paseo to have a cold drink with their families. They were identifiable by the different kinds of hats they wore and how dressed-up they were. The farm labourers, less interested in smart clothes, wore their caps or berets.

At the Romería too the space was meticulously divided. The property-owning classes occupied the rooms in the annexe to the Sanctuary. There they laid out their food and wine and attended to their guests, separating themselves from the rest of the public. Meanwhile the rancheros, tenants and labourers camped in the olive groves which surrounded the hermitage, eating their victuals. Together but not intermingled; conscientiously separate according to the distinct social differences that existed in the rigid social structure of the latifundismo system.[5]

Carnival

In the early 1960s Carnival began to return to its pre-war format in Alcalá, Benalup and a few other towns in the province, now with musical influences from the British and American pop music being played on the radio. There was plenty to sing about, with continuing poverty and poor working conditions, but direct criticism of the regime was avoided. In 1967 Carnival was officially banned outside in the capital, but continued underground.

Carnavaleros in Alcalá (Archivo Emilio González)

Christmas – Los Reyes

The 1960s saw Balthazar, Gaspar and Melchior, the three wise men, ride through the streets of Alcalá on 5 January for the first time, distributing sweets and small gifts to the children.

Cinema

The Cine Andalucía, which had opened in 1957, was lavishly furnished compared to its predecessors with a roof, a full-size screen and relatively comfortable seating. It offered alcalaínos, most of whom had no access to television let alone foreign holidays, a technicolor view of the outside world. Westerns and action movies were the most popular genres. When the lights went out the back row offered young couples an opportunity for intimacy away from the watchful eye of parents and neighbours.[61]

All foreign films continued to be dubbed into Spanish, and censorship was still applied under the guidance of the Catholic church, though it was relaxed slightly in 1963 when women's rights were formally acknowledged in law. Some Spanish films made during this period started to question gender roles, addressing the tension between tradition and modernity. The majority however continued to portray men and women in traditional gender roles, depicting happy family life as the norm.[62]

"Los Ranger's Black"

In the early 1960s the town's first authentic pop group was formed, Los Ranger's Black (sic). Their repertoire reflected the appeal of all things English in a country just emerging from the most repressive years of the dictatorship. British pop songs were starting to be played on Spanish radio. Mini-skirts, psychedelic shirts, patchouli oil, gin & tonic and American cigarettes were all the rage. Alcalá artist and sculptor Jesús Cuesta Arana, a big fan who designed their stage sets, wrote about them on his blog:

> In this [culture of modernity] the Rangers burst forth in Alcalá de los Gazules, which was used to a different kind of rancher. Four kids jumped on the sonic bandwagon of the times. It was like a kind of alcalaíno Beatles. They did more than cheer people up with their music and self-assurance; they brought fresh air and new sensations to an era of anxiety. They openly challenged the moralizing and hypocrisy that had never got the better of them. They travelled to Cádiz and many other pueblos, playing in concerts and at fairs.[63]

The name also reflects the anglophilia of the age. "Rangers" were rancheros, a common enough occupation around Alcalá. The superfluous apostrophe and the adjective following the noun were unimportant as hardly anyone spoke English. The band learned the lyrics phonetically, often having no idea what they were singing about. Founder member Manolo Caro wrote:

> The group was born in the years 1961-62... As well as a musical group it was an important youth movement. "Los Ranger's" wasn't just four people. It was practically the

whole of Alcalá's younger generation, a big percentage. Many people came to our gigs. They helped us set up the stage, carry the equipment, and even our distinguished friend Cuestarana painted some impressive "Tiffanys" [Art Nouveau-style backdrops]. *Our beloved drummer Juan Romero used to hit the roof when he went to get paid, because our entire fee had been spent on beer, wine and* pinchitos.[64]

"The cradle of Andalusian socialism"

As the years rolled by Franco's days were clearly numbered and the Spanish Socialist Workers' Party (PSOE) which had been in exile since the fall of the Second Republic began to prepare itself for the return to democracy. A group of young men from Alcalá played a significant role in this process, earning the town the epithet *"cuna de socialismo andaluz"*.

Luis Pizarro Medina was born in 1947. His uncle Francisco was one of those murdered by the Falangists after the coup, and his aunt Francisca had been paraded through the town with her head shaved after being forced to drink castor oil. He would eventually become Vice-Secretary of the PSOE and minister of governance and justice in the Junta de Andalucía.

Alfonso Perales Pizarro, born in 1954, was the nephew of Alcalá's first CNT member Juan Perales León, and his father had survived one of Franco's concentration camps in Huelva. He would be elected to Congress in 2004 and served in the PSOE government of José Luis Rodríguez Zapatero, helping to reform the statutes of autonomy for Andalucía, Valencia and Catalonia.

José Luis "Pepe" Blanco Romero, born in 1953, held the first PSOE membership card in the Province of Cádiz in 1971, when it was still illegal. He would become minister for the environment in the Andalusian parliament in 1996.

Francisco Aido Arroyo, born in 1952, would become in 1979 the first democratically elected mayor of Alcalá since February 1936. His daughter Bibiana Aido would become Spain's first minister of equal rights in 2008, during the Zapatero government.

All shared a restless zeal for social justice, and in 1970 they came under the influence of Antonio Guerrero, an electrician from Seville who had come to Alcalá to work on the construction of the flats at Los Larios. Guerrero introduced them to a group of his comrades in Seville (known as the "Capitán Vigueras" group after the street where their legal firm was based) including the future president of Spain, Felipe González, and the future president of the Junta de Andalucía, Manuel Chaves. There the alcalaínos were persuaded that lasting changes they sought would be better achieved via social reform than by revolution.

The Alcalá clan, as they became known, moved to Cádiz; Blanco to study education, Perales to study history and Pizarro to work in a finance company for SEAT. There they and their colleagues set up a secret discussion group in a student flat to argue about how to bring genuine social reform to Andalucía. They distributed leaflets in factories and working-class neighbourhoods, becoming gradually bolder until in 1974 Blanco was arrested and beaten up by the police. He had intended to go to a seminal PSOE meeting in Suresnes, a suburb of Paris, where the party would officially decide how to relaunch itself. Perales went in his place, along with Chaves. The reformists prevailed over the revolutionaries, Felipe González was named Secretary-General, and the

PSOE became the party that would dominate Spanish politics for much of the rest of the century.[65]

L-R: José Luis Blanco, Luis Pizarro, Manuel Chaves, Carlos Díaz, Rafael Román, Alfonso Perales

Line drawing of the Alameda by the author

CHAPTER 5 – 1979-2000

Spain is hereby established as a social and democratic State, subject to the rule of law, which advocates freedom, justice, equality and political pluralism as the highest values of its legal system. National sovereignty belongs to the Spanish people, from whom all state powers emanate.
(Article 1 of the Constitution of Spain, 1978)

Background

In April 1979 Spain held its first local elections since the Popular Front victory in 1936. Adolfo Suárez's UCD polled 31% of the vote, the PSOE led by Felipe González 28%, and the PCE 13%. The rest went to independents and regionalist parties.

Suárez resigned as Prime Minister in January 1981 and a month later, while his successor was being confirmed, 150 armed Civil Guards and soldiers led by Antonio Tejero burst into Parliament and held the congressmen hostage for 22 hours, proof of continuing opposition to reform. They eventually surrendered after the King gave a televised speech at midnight denouncing the attempted coup and urging the continuance of the democratic process, but the length of time he took to show his hand drew criticism from some quarters.

The UCD coalition eventually collapsed and a general election was held in October 1982. The PSOE won with a comfortable majority and went on to win the next three, before losing to José María Aznar's Partido Popular (PP) in 1996.

During this long period of political stability the country saw many reforms in line with the new Constitution: universal free education and healthcare, extensive improvements to the pension and social security systems, the legalisation of divorce, the establishment of family planning clinics, varying degrees of autonomy for the regions, and a partial legalisation of abortion. But the PSOE government failed to tackle fundamental and controversial issues such as the recovery of thousands of bodies buried without ceremony in unknown locations during the Civil War, the numerous fiscal and other privileges given to the Catholic Church, or deep-rooted corruption in the political and legislative system.

During the 1980s a wave of hedonism known as *la movida madrileña*, immortalised by the early films of Pedro Almodovar, followed the removal of strict censorship and other cultural restrictions. Madrid and other major cities were awash with pornography, prostitution, gay clubs, recreational drugs of all kinds, punk bands and various related phenomena guaranteed to upset the old regime, while the new one turned a blind eye. Its lasting legacy was a generation whose lives were blighted by drug addiction.

Andalucía was constituted as an autonomous community in 1981 with its own elected parliament and control over areas such as health and social care, education and environmental protection. It was governed by the PSOE continuously until 2017.

Spain joined the European Community (as the EU was then known) in 1986, when its GDP per capita was just 72% of the average among its members. The opening up of new export markets, along with substantial grants and loans to improve its infrastructure, helped contribute to an economic boom in Spain which lasted until an international recession in the early 1990s. Andalucía, being one of Spain's poorest regions, benefited substantially from regional development funds.

Local elections in Alcalá

The PSOE won the 1979 municipal election comfortably with 56% of the vote and eight councillors, compared to the UCD's 41% and five seats. The PCE received 74 votes, not enough for a seat on the council, and the large number of abstentions (42%) included CNT members who boycotted the poll.

The *Pacto de Olvido* reflected Spain's decision to deal with the horrific events that had taken place earlier in the century by pretending they had never happened. The first act of the new Ayuntamiento was to remove physical reminders of the fascist regime by changing the names of streets and squares that had been renamed after the coup to honour Nationalist leaders. To avoid controversy it was decided to restore them to what they had been familiarly known as before the Second Republic:

Calle Queipo de Llano – Calle Rio Verde
Calle General Mola – Calle los Pozos
Plaza General Varela - Plaza Santo Domingo
Plaza Generalísimo Franco – Alameda de la Cruz
Calle General Primo de Rivera – Calle Real
Plaza de Calvo Sotelo – Plaza Plazuela

Paseo de José Antonio – Paseo de la Playa
Calle de Carrero Blanco – Calle Constitución.[66]

The Ayuntamiento also voted to remove the Cross of the Fallen (*Cruz de los Caídos*) which stood next to the church in the Plaza Alta honouring those who had died fighting "for God and for Spain". This symbol of fascist triumphalism was pulled down and taken away to an unknown destination by council employees, without fuss or protest. But there was no attempt to install any kind of monument to the Popular Front mayor and his colleagues murdered in the coup of July 1936.

In 1979 a new law granted pension rights and other benefits to widows and families of war victims on both sides. To access these benefits they needed to be able to prove that the person had died as a result of the Civil War. Some claimants had never registered the deaths of their loved ones, but they were allowed to do so retro-spectively with the testimony of two witnesses. The death certificates were then presented to the Ayuntamiento which applied for assistance on their behalf, ten claims in all.[66]

Another new law awarded lifetime pensions to men unable to work because of war injuries, regardless of which side. Again the Ayuntamiento acted as a conduit between the townspeople and the state, processing claims on their behalf. Alcalá's veteran CNT leader Juan Perales León, who among other injuries had half his face blown away in 1938 while fighting for the government forces, finally received a pension more than forty years later.

In the next round of municipal elections (1983) the PSOE in-creased its share to 75% of the vote, with ten councillors, and the UCD's successor, a right-wing coalition known as the AP-PDP, held the other three seats. This dominance of the centre-left in Alcalá continued throughout the century, although during the late 1990s the Partido Andalucista, promoting greater autonomy for the region, temporarily gained support achieving 29% of the local vote in 1999.

The occupation of the Ayuntamiento

The Community Employment scheme (EC) referred to in the previous chapter continued during the transition to democracy, and in Alcalá the annual subsidy rose from 5 million pts in 1977 to 26 million in 1980. This steep increase was mainly due to pressure from the unions, notably the UGT and the Comisiones Obreras (CC-OO), both of which had close links with newly-elected councillors in the Ayuntamiento.

The CNT, which had been secretly revived in the late 1960s, was not represented on the Ayuntamiento and found itself excluded from negotiations when it came to the allocation of EC funds. Moreover the PSOE's strategy was to place the blame for mass unemployment firmly on the UCD government while continuing to work within its framework, whereas the CNT was pressing for more radical solutions, including the restoration of access to the resources of the forests, and agrarian reform to provide work on land that had been uncultivated since the 1950s. Some CNT members had voted for the PSOE despite the regional leaders' recommendation for abstention, believing that as they had all fought side by side in the past, the anarchists would not be sidelined with the return of democracy. But they were to be disappointed.

The CNT and other leftist organisations outside the PSOE continued to organise protests against chronic mass unemployment. Beginning in February 1978 there were several incidents of direct action in the Province, including the occupation of fincas to be "worked directly" (i.e. without a contract with the landowner), lock-ins (*encierros*) in town halls, and hunger strikes.

In 1979 the newly-elected mayors of several provincial towns met and agreed that the only legitimate way forward was to demand an increase in the employment subsidy, which they duly received. But this was a mere sticking-plaster. After a much-publicised hunger strike in Villamartin in the Sierra de Cádiz early in 1981, which went on for nearly a month, the government promised to guarantee four days work each week for all the jornaleros in Andalucía. However the next monthly payment to the

Alcalá Ayuntamiento was just 750,000 pts, the equivalent of €41 per worker in today's terms, nowhere near the promised amount.

The outcome was that on 15th May 1981 two hundred jornaleros, many of them CNT members, held a mass meeting and locked themselves inside the Ayuntamiento for a period of 17 days. Their demands were printed in the Diario de Cádiz:

> An assembly was held in which the campesinos made their demands clear. They demand that the landowners hire unemployed workers in numbers proportional to the hectares they possess. In addition they denounce the fact that more than 60% of the municipality's own land is in an uncultivated state, while unemployment reaches alarming levels with just two days a week of community employment.

The mayor promptly sent a telegram to the Civil Governor in Cádiz and the payment was increased to 950,000 pts, which still did not match the promised four days per week. The occupation continued, with local supporters taking in food and depositing funds into a bank account, and anarchist groups from as far away as Catalonia sending truckloads of supplies.

The protesters viewed the Ayuntamiento, as the owner of nine fincas, in the same light as the latifundistas whom councillors had themselves condemned for leaving their land unproductive. But the mayor continued to blame central government, pointing out that responsibility for maintaining the public fincas lay with ICONA, a central government agency, not the Ayuntamiento.

The occupation came to an end when the Ayuntamiento agreed to meet local landowners and try to mitigate the situation. For a while a few of them did employ more workers, but it hardly made a dent in the problem. Fields remain uncultivated, there were no changes to the management of the forests, and the Ayuntamiento came up with no innovative new schemes to create jobs; they continued to rely on EC subsidies, and were increasingly accused of using these funds to line the pockets of their own supporters.

On several occasions over the next two years groups of jornaleros tried to "work directly" on uncultivated land, but were seen off by the Guardia Civil. The Ayuntamiento gave its approval for a small group to work Laganes, one of the estates owned by the municipality, but it failed because the workers had no animals to transport firewood or charcoal (for which there was by now very little demand) the long distance into the town. This would be the last example of local people organising to take control of resources that had once been theirs by right.[5]

Rural Employment Plan

In 1986 the EC programme was replaced in Andalucía and Extremadura, the Spanish regions with the highest levels of rural employment, by the *Plan de Empleo Rural* (PER). It was intended to remove the element of discretion in the allocation of jobs; if you fulfilled certain criteria you were automatically eligible to register and apply for work. It also included training programmes, though with no guarantee of work afterwards. In Alcalá the PER was used in its first year to finance various road improvements, the resurfacing of the municipal park and the construction of the industrial estate on the Prado.

Like its predecessor the main use of the PER in Alcalá was to finance the cork harvest on fincas owned by the town. The distinction between the teams of corcheros who worked on private estates for a fixed rate and those working for the Ayuntamiento on a daily rate grew wider. The former were better paid, but the job was more demanding and they could not afford to spend time clearing the undergrowth or training apprentices. The latter involved going cap in hand to the mayor, which did not suit everyone, and the foremen often found themselves in charge of inexperienced men who had not worked together before as a team.[5]

The allocation of work contracts and other social benefits was entirely at the discretion of the mayor. He was given a list of those eligible and allocated jobs to names on the list, supposedly based on his knowledge of each family's economic situation. There were always more petitioners than jobs, and many people claimed that the allocation of funds was used as a means of social control to reward those who supported the party and punish those who didn't.

A similar situation existed with the awarding of contracts to local firms; if you weren't openly supporting the PSOE, critics claimed, you didn't get a look-in.

But the availability of relatively well-paid work and benefits for periods of unemployment meant that at long last, the great divide between the social classes in Alcalá began to narrow. Gone were the days of hunger and squalor, illiteracy, overcrowding and general hopelessness among the jornaleros. Working-class families now had running water, indoor toilets, a varied diet, free health-care, contraception, and access to the same clothes and consumer goods as their middle-class neighbours. "Today there is no difference between rich and poor" became a well-used (though decidedly inaccurate) aphorism.[5]

Healthcare and social security

Franco is often praised by his followers for introducing Spain's first health service and social security system: sickness insurance in 1942, old-age and disability insurance in 1947 and unemployment insurance in 1961. But they were all contribution-based and therefore only accessible to those with salaried posts or the self-employed with successful businesses.

For many alcalaínos, with no job security and long periods of forced unemployment, there was no possibility of meeting the cost of insurance contributions. For them the only form of assistance during the dictatorship had been the Church or the *Auxilio Social*, neither of which was impartial in its assessment of need.

The 1978 Constitution established the right to a social security system available to all, guaranteeing assistance during periods of unemployment or sickness, and a basic pension as a safety net for those with insufficient or non-existent contributions. The laws enabling these benefits were passed by the PSOE government in the early 1980s.

The Constitution also guaranteed the provision of healthcare to the entire population, publicly funded but co-existing alongside the private sector. Responsibility for health and social care was devolved to the regions and the *Servicio Andaluz de Salud* (SAS) was set up in 1986. Not long after the public health facilities in Alcalá moved from a small surgery in Calle José Tizón to their current building on the Paseo de la Playa (formerly a youth club). The "Consultorio" provided access to family doctors, routine tests and a range of minor surgical procedures, and a free ambulance service was contracted to take patients to the hospital in Puerto Real or Cádiz if required.

The Consultorio on the Paseo de la Playa

The effects of better and more accessible healthcare can be seen in the life expectancy statistics for Andalucía, which rose during the period covered by this chapter from around 70 for men and 76 for women to 77 and 83 respectively, among the highest in Europe. During the same period, thanks largely to the removal of restrictions on contraception along with better educational and employment opportunities for women, the birth rate fell from over three children per couple to 1.4, while infant mortality rates fell from 13 per 1000 live births to less than four. The average age for a woman to have her first child rose from 28 to 31.5, and the number of babies born to unmarried couples rose from virtually zero to 15%.[67]

Local businesses

In the 1980s it became profitable to raise dairy goats, especially a high-yield breed native to the Sierra de Cádiz known as *payoya*. A co-operative was set up which purchased milk from farmers who could bring it to a collection point in the town on a daily basis. But lack of transport and the poor state of roads in the campo, particularly during the rainy season, made this difficult for some farmers who instead turned to making cheese at home or using the milk to fatten pigs.

In 1998 an enterprising young ranchero named Jorge Puerto had the idea of making high-quality cheeses from the milk of payoya goats, buying it directly from their owners. He set up a factory on the Polígono La Palmosa which in the 21st century would become one of the town's most successful small businesses, the award-winning Quesería El Gazul.

Another business which prospered during this period was Legumbres Pedro, whose founder Pedro Benítez started by purchasing chickpeas from local growers, cleaning them by hand and selling them to shops and restaurants in the town. By the 1980s he had extended the range to include lentils and other legumes and was supplying supermarket chains and the catering trade. The business would move from premises next to the family home in San Antonio to its present location, a purpose-built factory on the Polígono, in 2008.

Radio Hogar on Calle Rio Verde sold furniture and electrical appliances and expanded to meet the growing demand for televisions, washing machines and refrigerators. The store offered a scheme whereby you could pay in a small amount each week until you had enough to buy what you wanted. This was considered preferable to buying goods on credit.

SuperArcos in Santo Domingo was the first self-service supermarket in the pueblo. The company was founded in Arcos de la Frontera in 1977 and soon had stores all over the province, selling locally-produced as well as imported goods. But most people remained loyal to their little corner-shops, which served as a meeting-place to catch up on local gossip as well somewhere convenient to buy provisions in the small quantities needed for the day.

There were still a few foraging activities which alcalaínos could undertake on their own account; as well as the usual snails and edible plants to sell in the town, there was a growing market for wild mushrooms such as chanterelles and boletus, which were flown from Jerez airport to arrive fresh in the markets of France or Germany.

Housing

The urban area of Alcalá expanded considerably during this period. The building of dwellings (mainly flats) for those who could obtain a mortgage continued, and it was also common to self-build, especially by men who worked in the construction industry elsewhere. They would pool their skills and build their houses little by little over the years. These houses were mainly located on the outskirts of the pueblo, including the lower half of the steep hill known as La Salá (Calle Nuestra Señora de los Santos).

In the 1980s an estate of over a hundred single-family homes was built at the bottom of that hill, on flat land known as El Prado next to the River Barbate. They were available to rent at subsidised rates under the VPO scheme.

Self-built homes on La Salá and the VPO estate on El Prado

The availability of new affordable housing had a detrimental effect on the area around the Plaza Alta, traditionally occupied by the lowest social class, which became depopulated and many buildings fell into ruin. A restoration programme financed by the Junta de Andalucía would eventually turn some of them back into habitable dwellings with VPO status.

Depopulation of the campo also continued steadily and by the end of the 20th century less than 10% of alcalaínos lived outside the pueblo, compared to around half at its start.

Religion and the Church

The removal of religious indoctrination from state schools appears to have had little effect on people's beliefs during this period. In 2000, 83% of the population self-declared as Catholic (although 43% rarely if ever went to church). It would be the subsequent generation that began to turn their back on the Church; by 2015 26% of Spaniards identified as non-believers, and more than two-thirds never attended Mass. The proportions were significantly higher in younger age groups.[68]

The religious brotherhoods in Alcalá continued to exercise influence in the community, trying to attract younger members by organising special events for them. In 1996 the Cofradia del Nazareno, faced with the difficulty of finding a band for its Easter processions, decided to form its own. They recruited twenty boys from the pueblo, acquired some drums, and practised for two months in a disused abattoir before leading the Holy Thursday procession accompanying the statue of Christ on the Cross, wearing the tunics and capes of the Brotherhood. Brass and woodwind instruments were purchased the following year and the band evolved into the Musical Group of Our Father Jesus of Nazareth, performing not only during Holy Week but at other events in the church calendar throughout the year.[69]

Agrupación Musical Nuestro Padre Jesús Nazareno

Holy Week poster, sponsored by a bank

EU membership

In 1986 Spain joined the European Community, as it was then known, and almost immediately the region saw an explosion of acronymic agencies with the aims of creating rural employment, protecting the environment, and improving the productivity of the land – aims that occasionally came into conflict. The Common Agricultural Policy benefited big landowners and agribusinesses far more than rancheros. For example, there were subsidies for large-scale arable production and breeding fighting bulls, but not for small market gardens or working mules. Health and safety restrictions put an end to some small-scale domestic enterprises such as the use of unpasteurised milk for cheese-making. It also became illegal to leave animal carcasses out on the mountains to be eaten by vultures, a practice that had been carried out since time immemorial, because of the BSE scare; farmers now had to pay for them to be safely disposed of.

But there were plenty of funds to improve the quality of the forests, and these created employment for local people, as did the construction of the A-381 dual carriageway from Jerez to Los Barrios which commenced in 1996. It was distinguished by its "green tunnels" which allowed animals in the Natural Park to cross safely and reduced the incidence of inbreeding.

EU membership sparked a second wave of emigration as young alcalaínos took advantage of freedom of movement and the Erasmus university exchange scheme to work and study in other member states. England was a particularly popular destination, possibly became of all the cultural references they had absorbed while growing up; it already felt familiar to them.

The Alcornocales Natural Park

From the mid-1980s the government set about establishing a number of protected regions of special environmental interest, and the *Parque Natural de los Alcornocales* (PNA) was established in 1989. It was not welcomed by all alcalaínos. A plethora of new regulations and restrictions on activities within the PNA were introduced, some of which reduced the viability of small-scale agricultural or livestock farming still further. Even the name was regarded with contempt; the locals called the cork-oaks *chaparros*, not *alcornoques*.

The new regulations also had a negative effect on the various foraging activities which were the primary source of income for those excluded from the PER, as they now had to apply for permits. These now included the collection of cones from the recently planted pines, which were sent to Barbate for the extraction of pine-nuts; palm leaves, dried in the sun and woven into baskets; and heather, which was made into sun-hats and beach-mats for sale on the Costa del Sol. Digging up roots to make into briar pipes was declared an incompatible activity because it contributed to soil erosion.

Nonetheless a few people carried on harvesting the resources of the montes (including rabbits), which they regarded as "belonging to no-one and to everyone". Many of the guards employed on the estates were friends or relatives of the foragers, and tolerated these activities as long as they weren't too blatant. If they caught someone, they let them off provided they left the estate straight away. But other guards took their job more seriously and administered unrestrained corporal punishment.

One of the stated aims of setting up the PNA was to make the natural environment accessible to visitors. A picnic area was set up near the foot of Picacho, a few official trails were designated for walkers, and Camping Gazul offered year-round accommodation in Patriste complete with pony-trekking. A residential facility, the *Aula de Picacho*, was built to provide summer camps for schoolchildren, which included environmental awareness classes.

But in reality open access was only viable on land owned by the town not designated for hunting. Private landowners erected fences and gates on public rights of way with impunity, and 90% of the PNA remains inaccessible to the public to this day.

In 1990 measures were formalised to prevent forest fires within the PNA and a regional operations centre was built in Alcalá, with specialist firefighters using helicopters to detect and extinguish fires.

Hunting

Shooting wild animals became by far the most lucrative tourist activity in the PNA. There are two kinds of licences: *caza major* - deer, wild boar, ibex and mouflon (the latter two introduced recently) and *caza menor* - rabbits, hares and birds of all kinds. Hunters must join an official federation and obtain a membership card, which includes insurance and which is needed when applying for a firearms licence from the Guardia Civil, along with various other documents and a medical certificate. Licence fees are paid to the Junta de Andalucía, which is responsible for maintaining healthy populations of prey animals and deciding the seasons and number of kills permitted for each species.

In 1979 there were ten zones (*cotos*) licensed for *caza mayor* in the municipality of Alcalá, one-third of the total area. Seven of the owners lived in Jerez, including the heir to the Las Lomas estate discussed in an earlier chapter. They built well-appointed lodges to accommodate the organised hunting parties arriving from Spanish cities and increasingly from abroad, as well as their own friends and families. They also built more humble dwellings for gamekeepers and security guards. All grazing by domestic animals was excluded.

Until the 1990s local societies were excluded from hunting *caza mayor* but could obtain licences for *caza menor*. This included Alcalá's *Asociacíon de Cazadores Nuestra Señora de los Santos*, and clubs from other towns in the province. Unlicensed hunting also took place, notably by *moteros* who went out on their motor-bikes with a pack of greyhounds and could catch up to five hundred rabbits in one night, which over the course of the year more than compensated for any fines and beatings incurred.

"La movida alcalaína"

During the 1980s the culture of sex, drugs and rock'n'roll that had begun in Madrid rippled across the country and Alcalá became a social hub for young people in the district, offering numerous diversions such discos, bars and the easy availability of recreational drugs.

Alcalá's first discotheque was opened in 1980 by Paco Pizarro, next to his family's restaurant on the Paseo:

The inauguration of Discoteca Pizarro was a success, because at that time it was the only disco within a 60km radius. Word quickly got round and youngsters arrived from all over the Province. In the early days the disco served as a venue where young people could meet and get to know each other ... within a year of opening it resulted in several weddings.

The disco was full every night, but sadly drugs became a part of the nightlife and it turned into a less wholesome and innocent place. In addition, the fashions which were permeating youth culture were changing so quickly that suddenly everyone wanted to hear heavy metal instead of the old dance numbers, and it was no longer so laid-back. People danced individually to the new rhythms, there was no time for romantic ballads, and as a witness to this evolution I couldn't help feeling sad, because just as the music was changing so were the clothes, the customs, the way of relating to each other and of viewing the world. With some of the trends, punk for example, they became quite badly-behaved ... With the arrival of drugs in Spain many young lives were ruined, partly because of their naivety and partly because of the desire to try new experiences ...

For these reasons some parents stopped allowing their children to go to the disco. They were afraid they would pick up bad habits, I imagine, but the kids didn't take any notice. Then I think they must have started complaining to the authorities, because plain-clothes police started to turn up, mixing with the crowds ...[48]

An open-air disco operated during the 1980s in the Plaza de Toros, which must have been a real treat for the neighbours. Also during the early '80s Alcalá had its own radio station, Radio Potoco (named after a famous bullfighter from the 1920s), broadcasting local news and music.

The ban on contraception in Spain was lifted in 1978 but there was no sex education in schools and no family planning service; the result of new-found sexual freedom was a rise in the number of unplanned pregnancies and backstreet abortions (termination became legal in 1985 but only under very limited circumstances).

The biggest growth industry in the area during the 1980s was smuggling drugs across the Mediterranean from Morocco and onwards into the rest of Europe. A few people in the town succumbed to the temptation of easy money and became part of the supply chain, driving around the town in fancy cars and hardly bothering to conceal their activities. The scale of operations became too extensive for the Guardia Civil to handle, and there were rumours that some were themselves on the traffickers' payroll.

On returning to Alcalá after a few years away, Paco Pizarro noted:

> *I saw how some young people had got involved with the world of drugs, especially heroin, and had turned from being studious youngsters into human wrecks. For example an old friend, very pretty, who had been a hard-working student and written beautiful poetry, had become "hooked" and lost everything, even resorting to prostitution to buy the drug that would end her life.*[48]

Sport

Improving the town's sports facilities was high on the Ayuntamiento's agenda. It was believed that encouraging young people to take up sport helped distract them from the temptations of drugs. An indoor sports centre was built on the Pico del Campo, and the football ground on the Prado was given an all-weather surface. A large open-air swimming pool on the Prado replaced the smaller one behind the Hotel Rey Gazul (now Hotel San Jorge), and soon became a popular venue not only for swimming but Sunday afternoon picnics for the whole family.

Competitions with neighbouring towns in soccer, basketball and handball were popular. The sporting association U.D. Alchoyano was founded in 1990, sponsored by local businesses and supporting teams of all ages using volunteer trainers, organising tournaments, and providing kit for those who couldn't afford to buy their own.

Municipal swimming pool on the Prado

Women's lives

The feminist movement that took place in much of the Western world during the 1970s and '80s had little impact on the lives of women in rural communities such as Alcalá. Their lives were very much centred around cooking, cleaning, going to Mass, supporting their husbands and raising children - the old Francoist role model for appropriate feminine behaviour. Women who lived in the campo had the additional tasks of maintaining the vegetable garden and looking after the pigs and poultry. Many of them were widows or lived alone much of the time, as their husbands worked away from the area.

Machismo was enshrined in the law as well as in daily life. Until 1981 women could not sign any form of legal contract without their husband's permission. There was no comprehensive law relating to domestic violence until 2004, and the Gender Equality Act, outlawing discrimination in the workplace and other areas, was not passed until 2007.

One woman interviewed in the early 1980s by Jerome Mintz in Benalup complained:

> *Women here are not liberated. We can't go out alone, we have to go with our husbands. Almost all husbands are jealous and ignorant. We can't wear trousers or a shirt. I put on a pair of slacks once and he ripped them up. I cried from being so angry. They think they work harder than us, but we look after the children and clean the house...[19]*

There is no reason to believe things were any different in Alcalá. It was considered unfeminine and treacherous to complain about your lot, there were no formal support mechanisms or opportunities for women to speak with a collective voice, and few would run the risk of becoming the object of gossip. If a woman wanted any kind of professional career, she stayed single.[70]

Women were initially excluded from applying for paid work under the Community Employment programme and its successors because they were not considered to be breadwinners. After 1990 the Ayuntamiento started giving contracts to women to work in the montes clearing scrub and spraying pesticides, unpopular jobs, possibly as a means of deterring them from registering as unemployed. Later they switched to offering unskilled work such as street-sweeping or weeding the municipal gardens.[5]

The Adult Education Centre (see below) evolved to play an important role in the lives of women, offering informal advice and support when needed, organising talks on women's rights issues, and giving them the confidence to take part in activities outside the home.

The *Asociación de Mujeres de Alcalá de los Gazules* (AMAG) was founded in 1990, offering women the opportunity to take part in social and cultural activities in the town, access to vocational training programmes, and workshops on a wide variety of topics.

The Adult Education Centre

At the beginning of the 1980s the Junta de Andalucía launched a programme to teach literacy skills to people who had had little or no formal education. The region had the highest illiteracy rates in the country; 12% couldn't read or write at all, and over a third couldn't fill in a form or understand a contract. Rates were much higher among women, since in the past it had not been considered worth spending money educating them.[71]

This inspired Mercedes Sánchez Erdozain and Inmaculada Almagro, both unemployed teachers from Alcalá, to open a school for adults in the pueblo. The Ayuntamiento allocated them a room in a disused building in Calle Lepanto, but there was no furniture or heating. Inma and Mercedes resolved the first problem by going round the town collecting old broken chairs and tables that had been thrown out. These were restored and painted in a workshop next to the school, which continued to operate for many years.

The initial attempt to attract students by putting up posters failed miserably so the two women went knocking on doors, trying to persuade their neighbours of the benefits of being able to read and write. They met with some resistance from men who didn't think it was appropriate for their wives to neglect their household duties for such trivial pursuits, and there was reluctance on the part of others to admit they didn't have these basic skills. The school opened in 1984 with just five students, all women.

When winter arrived they had to heat the room the old-fashioned way, with charcoal braziers under circular tables. They set about making curtains and tablecloths to keep in the heat. This was the origin of a sewing workshop which not only produced material benefits but also formed a welcoming social group for women outside the home. By the end of the first year there were forty students and a third teacher, Maribel Perales, joined the team.

The Centre went from strength to strength over the years and eventually occupied all five floors of the building, offering classes in a range of subjects including cookery, pottery, photography, local history, and preparation for taking the driving test. Along with its sister organisation, Jacaranda Gazul, it revived old customs and recipes typical of the area such as the preparation of *gazpacho caliente*, organised excursions and social events, and ran workshops on health, consumer rights and issues specifically affecting women.

Dance class at the Adult Education Centre, 1991

The Lorca plays

The Adult Education Centre had its own drama group, Teatro el Castillo, and staged eight plays by Federico García Lorca, Andalucia's most celebrated playwright. They were directed by Paco Pizarro, who had some experience of the theatre. None of the cast had any previous acting experience and a few had difficulty reading the script, but they could all identify strongly with the emotional content of the plays.

The fifth production was *Blood Wedding*, a tragedy set in rural Andalucía about a family feud. After several months rehearsing it was performed in the Beaterio, where it was a great success. They repeated the performance in nearby towns until word reached the ears of the director of culture in the Cádiz provincial government, who was so impressed with the alcalaínos' performance that they were chosen to represent the province in a competition organised by the Junta de Andalucía, to be held at a newly-opened theatre in Almería. The cast, some of whom had never travelled far from home before, were put up in a four-star hotel for a week and had the time of their lives. They went on to win first prize.[48]

Performance of 'Boda de Sangre' at the Beaterio, 1992

Flamenco in Alcalá

Alcalá is located deep in flamenco territory and well before the genre became internationally popular it was regularly heard in bars and *peñas* within the pueblo, at fairs and festivals and in the streets. The tradition, with its distinctive styles of singing, dancing, guitar-playing and complex rhythms, was kept alive mainly by settled gipsy families, of which there were several in the town. One family was headed by Sebastian Monje "El Cuco", a blacksmith who had a forge in Calle Nuestra Señora de los Santos in the 1940s.[7] His son went to work in San Fernando, birthplace of José Monje Cruz, better known as Camarón de la Isla, one of the world's most celebrated flamenco singers until his premature death in 1992. Their relationship isn't clear but there is still a singer in Alcalá today who is said to be a cousin of Camarón.

José Monje Cruz, "Camarón de la Isla"

Thanks largely to Camarón, guitarist Paco de Lucía and their generation, flamenco saw a popular revival in the 1970s and concerts were held regularly in the Cine Andalucía and in the municipal park. Paco Pizarro's bar on the Paseo was a favourite meeting place for visiting musicians.[48] Nonetheless, according to an article in the ABC newspaper Camarón refused to play a gig in the Cine Andalucía in July 1975 because there were too few people in the audience. He apparently fled over the rooftops and the organiser had to refund the tickets.[72]

Alejandro Sanz

The Alcalá connections of Alejandro Sanz are much better documented than those of Camarón. He was born Alejandro Sánchez Pizarro in Madrid in 1968, but his mother María was part of Alcalá's extensive Pizarro family and the boy spent his school holidays there. His father was a guitarist from Algeciras and a close friend of Paco de Lucía's father. Alejandro started playing flamenco as a boy but soon started writing his own songs and developed a more commercial style. His recording career took off in 1992 and he went on to become one of the biggest pop stars of the Americas, winning countless Grammy awards and selling more records in more countries than anyone else in the Spanish-speaking world. But he has always kept in touch with his Alcalá roots, giving a concert on the football ground in 2010 and attending the inauguration of a street named after him in 2019. A Sanz-related visitor centre is due to open on the Plaza Alta in 2020.

Viviendo de Prisa, first album by Alejandro Sanz

Fairs and Festivals

Carnival

Carnival in Alcalá returned to its pre-Franco format after his death. After 1977, when censorship was removed, the verses written and performed by the *chirigotas* became bawdy and sexually explicit. For a few years nothing was taboo – bestiality, incest, adultery, promiscuity, homosexuality. There was no longer a requirement to get the approval of the subject of the humour. However, although there was the opportunity for more overt political content, the lyricists were still cautious about offending authority.[19]

In Cádiz city, Carnival includes a competition for the best group in each category. Strict rules are imposed on the composition of different kinds of groups and their presentations. The contest attracts hundreds of groups from all over the Province, all eager to reach the finals held in the Falla Theatre. Those who prefer to perform in the streets rather than follow the rules and perform for the judges are known as *ilegales* (unofficial rather than illegal).

In 1981 a chirigota from Alcalá, "Los Esparragueros" (the asparagus-gatherers), directed by Domingo Ruiz, won 4th prize in the Provincial section. Shortly afterwards Alcalá introduced its own competition, though on a much smaller scale. The first such event was held in the high school, and the winners were the chirigota "Los Nenes Caca", which roughly translates as "the shitty kids". But the real action, then as now, was in the bars, on the Alameda or on the Paseo.

Other elements of Carnival were a masked ball with a live band, and a humorous fancy dress parade for people of all ages, with cash prizes for the best costumes.

Los Esparragueros

Los Nenes Caca

Many of the songs were written by men about women, some of them quite cruel and personal. Very few women were actively involved other than helping to make the costumes, though the Adult Education Centre participated with an all-female chirigota one year. However a singer from Benalup, Isabel, composed many lyrics from a female perspective. She could not read or write, but held them all in her memory:

> ... But now he gets drunk to make me suffer
> I've been married three months, my savings are gone
> And I curse the hour we met.
> I came home the other day, and he seemed much changed;
> He grabbed the bottle and put it away...
> ...He told me "I can't wait for you to die
> So I'll have some peace
> And all the money I earn, I'll spend on wine..."[19]

San Jorge

The celebrations in honour of the town's patron saint took off after Franco's death, merging with what remained of the spring livestock fair, with stalls selling food and drink, live music and dancing for three or four days around 23rd April, St George's Day. The central feature was the *suelta de vaquillas;* heifers from fighting bull stock were released on the Plaza Alta and ran through the streets to the Alameda, accompanied by young and not-so-young men keen to display their courage and skill.

It was an event that turned the social hierarchy of Alcalá on its head, being held in the most stigmatised part of town. The well-to-do had to climb the hill to the Plaza Alta and jostle for position with their employees, whose wives and mothers brought chairs from home and settled in the "gallery" along the side of the Church.

> ... Once a year it was not the labourer who had to go to
> the campo and scrape a living, collecting snails,
> poaching or picking wild asparagus who was the main
> protagonist. Now it was one of the fundamental resources

of the latifundista livestock-breeders, the cow, which had to climb to this emblematic place; those days when the crumbling dwellings were festooned with flags and bunting, and all, absolutely all of the local sectors, at one or other hour of the day, went up to the Plaza Alta. The civil authorities, the priests and the military participated in the service organised inside the church. Afterwards, if they wanted to continue celebrating outside, they had to mix with the people. There were no segregated places for them, it was the only local festival where they were not physically separated.[5]

The Feria and Romería

The September fair in honour of the Virgin was the main summer holiday for working people, who would enjoy themselves to the full during their week off. It was a noisy affair, with brass bands in the mornings, rock bands in the evenings, and the music from the dodgems, roundabouts and Ferris wheel growing louder each year. But it retained its Andalusian flavour, with men and women dressing up in their *trajes de gitano* to dance sevillanas and ride up and down on their magnificent horses, culminating in the overnight pilgrimage through the countryside to the Sanctuary where the festivities continued for another week.

In 2000 the fair moved from the Paseo to a purpose-built site on Monte Ortega, where there was room for the full range of fair-ground attractions as well as the ever-growing number of marquees. At the same time the date was moved to the last week of August to avoid overlapping with the Romería, which took place the weekend before María's saints' day, 12th September.

Nuestra Señora de los Santos

Postscript

When the winds of change blow, some people build walls, others build windmills. – Chinese proverb

On the eve of the Millennium the people of Alcalá celebrated *nochevieja* in the usual way with their enormous family meals, eating a grape for each stroke of midnight then going into the street to watch the fireworks light up the heavens. Few would have imagined that in a few years' time satellites circulating up there alongside the Virgin, the saints and the souls of the departed would enable them to communicate with each other across the globe via tiny rectangular devices that would fit in their pocket, powered by energy from the wind and sun.

Most of them would have assumed that the winds of change would continue to be favourable, improving their lives and those of their children, whose education had been so heavily invested in over the previous two decades.

But within ten years a brutal financial crisis that was none of their doing would bring mass unemployment, pay cuts, evictions and another wave of emigration, this time by educated twenty-somethings heading for the UK where they believed the streets were paved with gold.

With the resilience built from one hundred years of solidarity, those left behind would handle adversity with the aid of mutual support - strong family bonds and a deeply ingrained sense of community - and an enviable ability to put their cares to one side at fairs and festivals and live for the moment.

As I write this at the beginning of 2020, I can see that some things haven't changed. Alcalaínos still cross themselves as they pass the replica of the Virgin up the road, and still place votive offerings in the Sanctuary. They still largely shun the supermarket in favour of the corner shop. The mules still bring the cork down from the hills, the pueblo's numerous cockerels still crow at seemingly random hours, and Camarón's cousin still warbles away on the hill behind our house. The universal use of Whatsapp hasn't removed the need to stop and chat on the street every time you see someone you know, especially if there's a baby to coo over. Teenagers still link arms with their grandparents to walk slowly up and down the Paseo on summer evenings. People still collect wild asparagus and tagarninas to sell on the street. The Ayuntamiento is still dominated by the PSOE, which polled over 70% of the vote in last year's municipal elections. And the wilful Levante still comes out of nowhere, stealing the washing from the line, bending the trees double and rattling the blinds ...

References

1   Las ordenanzas municipales de 1900, I-V. Ismael Almagro Montes de Oca, *Historia de Alcalá de los Gazules* (blog) 2016.

2   Alcalá en los albores del siglo XX. Manuel Pérez Regordan, *Revista de Apuntes Históricos* 1983.

3   La sociedad de Alcalá en las vísperas de la guerra civil. Juan Pedro Romero Benítez, *Apuntes Históricos y de nuestro Patrimonio* 2017.

4   Desgracio por incendio de chozas y cortijos en el campo. Ismael Almagro Montes de Oca, *Historia de Alcalá de los Gazules* 2015.

5   *Los Camperos: Territorios, usos sociales y percepciones en un "espacio natural" andaluz.* Agustín Coca Pérez, Fundación Blas Infante 2008.

6   *Lamento Campesino: Un siglo crucial en la historia de Alcalá de los Gazules (1860-1960).* Guillermo García Jiménez, Publicaciones del Sur 1994.

7   *Lecturas e imágines alcalaínas.* Juan Leiva Sánchez, Publicaciones del Sur 2015.

8   Extract from a speech in tribute to the muleteers of Alcalá by Agustín Coca Pérez, July 2019.

9   *The Anarchists of Casas Viejas.* Jerome R. Mintz, Chicago University Press 1982.

10 La jornada laboral en Alcalá de los Gazules. Ismael Almagro Montes de Oca, *Historia de Alcalá de los Gazules* October 2019.

11 Eléctrica Nuestra Señora de los Santos - una empresa centenaria. Gabriel Almagro Montes de Oca, *Historia de Alcalá de los Gazules* October 2017.

12 El cine en Alcalá. Juan Manuel Muñoz Fernández-Armenta, *Revista de Apuntes Históricos* 2002.

13 Proyectos de escuela pública en Alcalá en el siglo XX (I). Jaime Guerra Martínez, *Historia de Alcalá de los Gazules* May 2015.

14 Una visita al Beaterio. Fabio, *Diario de Cádiz* May 1917.

15 Letter to *El Socialista*, Diego Valle Regife, June 1887.

16 La mortalidad infantil en Alcalá entre 1916 y 1921. Pablo Molanes Pérez & Ana María Sainz Otero, *Historia de Alcalá de los Gazules* January 2014.

17 Laskut, visión sobre el clamor y el entorno. Romero D. Fran, *Apuntes Históricos y de Nuestro Patrimonio* 2014.

18 Memoria de Puelles y Espinosa sobre el estado antipalúdico de Alcalá de los Gazules. Pablo Molanés Pérez, *Historia de Alcalá de los Gazules* 2015.

19 *Carnival Song and Society: Gossip, sexuality and creativity in Andalusia.* Jerome R. Mintz, Berg 1997.

20 Crónicas del ambiente alcalaíno (VI). *Historia de Alcalá de los Gazules* April 2018.

21 El estado de la Parroquia en 1920. Ismael Almagro Montes de Oca, *Historia de Alcalá de los Gazules* December 2017.

22 La restauración de la Iglesia de la Victoria: La historia se repite. Ismael Almagro Montes de Oca, *Historia de Alcalá de los Gazules* March 2019.

23 La Guerra de Marruecos y la Cruz de los Caidos. Ismael Almagro Montes de Oca, *Historia de Alcalá de los Gazules* August 2018.

24 The political mobilization of Catholic women in Spain's Second Republic: The CEDA 1931-6. Samuel Pearce, *Journal of Contemporary History* 45(1), 2010.

25 Juan Perales León, anarquista de Alcalá de los Gazules. J. Carlos Perales Pizarro, *Todos los Nombres* (website) 2013.

26 Don Antonio Gallego Visglerio, Alcalde Republicano de Alcalá de los Gazules. Fusilado en Julio de 1936. J, Carlos Perales Pizarro, *Apuntes Históricos y Patrimonio* 2003.

27 Mercados de abastos en el siglo XX. Jaime Guerra Martínez, *Revista de Apuntes Históricos* 1993.

28 El urinario público. Jaime Guerra Martínez, *Revista de Apuntes Históricos* 1995.

29 El origen del campo de fútbol en el Prado. Ismael Almagro Montes de Oca, *Historia de Alcalá de los Gazules* June 2018.

30 Proyectos de escuela pública en Alcalá del siglo XX. Jaime Guerra Martínez, *Historia de Alcalá de los Gazules* 2015.

31 Las elecciones de febrero de 1936 en Alcalá de los Gazules y el nuevo Ayuntamiento frentepopulista. Juan Pedro Romero Benítez, *Apuntes Históricos y de Nuestro Patrimonio* 2019.

32 Alcalá de los Gazules: Golpe de Estado Julio de 1936. J. Carlos Perales Pizarro, *Todos los Nombres* (website).

33 *La Historia del Movimiento Liberador de España en la Provincia de Cádiz. Eduardo* Juliá Tellez, Cerón 1944.

34 Francisca Pizarro Torres (1910-1989). Juana María Malia Vera, *Apuntes Históricos y de Patrimonio* 2006.

35 El 18 de julio de 1936 en Alcalá de los Gazules: Vispera del golpe cívico militar y represión. Agustín Coca Pérez, *Revista de Apuntes Históricos* 2011.

36 Ana Jiménez. J. Carlos Perales Pizarro, *Apuntes Históricos y Patrimonio* 2004.

37 Habilitados Nacionales - Secretarios, Interventores y Tesoreros de la Administración Local fusilados en la Guerra Civil.

38 La toma de la Sauceda. Ismael Almagro Montes de Oca, *Historia de Alcalá de los Gazules* July 2017.

39 La Guerra Civil en Alcalá: Breve crónica de un soldado alcalaíno en el Frente. Ismael Almagro Montes de Oca, *Historia de Alcalá de los Gazules* January 2013.

40 Alcalaínos en la Guerra Civil (I). Ismael Almagro Montes de Oca, *Historia de Alcalá de los Gazules* October 2019.

41 Wikipedia: *Ley de Responsabilidades Políticas.*

42 After the Civil War: Spain's hunger years. Barbara Lamplugh, personal blog 2017.

43 A vueltas con la justicia: Un caso histórico de un asesinato en Alcalá de los Gazules. Francisco Jiménez Vargas-Machuca, *Apuntes Históricos y de Patrimonio* 2016.

44 Comandante Abril. Carlos Torres Montañés, *Territorio Maquis: Historias, biografías y sucesos de aquellos años,* Asociación Gavilla Verde.

45 4,427 Spanish names against Nazi barbarism in Mauthausen. *El País,* 10 August 2019.

46 El Alcalá de mitad del Siglo XX. Francisco Teodoro Sánchez Vera, *Apuntes Históricos y de Nuestro Patrimonio* 2014.

47 Niños de los cincuenta. Manuel Jiménez Vargas-Machuca, *Alcalá de los Gazules* (blog) 2004.

48 *Tío Paco.* Francisco Pizarro, Montagud Editores 2013.

49 Eléctrica Nuestra Señora de los Santos III. Jaime Guerra Martínez, *Historia de Alcalá de los Gazules* November 2017.

50 La escuela rural: de los maestros de campo a las escuelas unitarias. José Luis Blanco Romero, *Revista de Apuntes Históricos* 2013.

51 El cine en Alcalá. Juan Manuel Muñoz Fernandez-Armenta, *Revista de Apuntes Históricos* 2002.

52 Forty Years of Censorship. *El País in English,* 30 December 2013.

53 *Fear and Loathing in la Liga.* Sid Lowe, Vintage 2014.

54 La subasta de los cuartos para la Romería. Ismael Almagro Montes de Oca, *Historia de Alcalá de los Gazules* August 2014.

55 Sueños de niños. Manuel Guerra Martínez, *Apuntes Históricos* 2014.

56 Tejidos Perales. Recuerdos y Añoranzas. J. Carlos Perales Pizarro, *Apuntes Históricos* 2017.

57 Tierra de Mujeres 9 - La invisibilidad de la mujer del mundo rural. Salustiano Gutierrez, *Desde la Historia de Casas Viejas* (blog) January 2020.

58 Bendición de unas viviendas. Diario de Cádiz 1967, published in *Historia de Alcalá de los Gazules* October 2017.

59 La creación del Instituto (1963-68). Jaime Guerra Martínez, *Apuntes Históricos* 2017.

60 Sobre las ferias de los 70. *Historia de Alcalá de los Gazules* August 2015.

61 Pablo Coca ahonda en la historia cinematográfica gaditana con el documental "Cine Andalucía". *Fundación Audiovisual Pública Andaluza* (website) November 2019.

62 *A cinema of contradiction: Spanish film in the 1960s.* Sally Faulkner, Edinburgh University Press 2006.

63 Cuando sonaron los Rangers. Jesús Cuesta Arana (personal blog) 2011.

64 Breve Resumen de la Historia de Los Ranger's. Manuel Caro Rios, *Alcalá de los Gazules* (blog) 2016.

65 La semilla del electricista. Pedro Ingelmo, *Diario de Cádiz* 10 April 2011.

66 La Memoria Histórica en los Ayuntamientos Democráticos de Alcalá de los Gazules 1979-1983. Juan Pedro Romero Benítez, *Apuntes Históricos* 2020.

67 Junta de Andalucía – Estadística y Cartografía (website).

68 Centro de Investigaciones Sociológicas (CIS), barometers of social indicators (website).

69 Agrupación Musical Nuestro Padre Jesús Nazareno (blog).

70 *Tierra de Mujeres*. María Sánchez, Seix Barral 2019.

71 La alfabetización fue el revulsivo para la emancipación de la mujer andaluza. Pedro Ingelmo, *Diario de Cádiz* 15 February 2020.

72 Camarón de la Isla en Alcalá. *Historia de Alcalá de los Gazules* March 2012.

Printed in Great Britain
by Amazon

73026287R00098